Remembering

Who You Are

A Healing Personal Spiritual Journey

John Aversano

John Aversano
PO Box 331
Saddle River, New Jersey 07458-0331
USA
201-825-3734
E-mail: john@Spiritual-Journey.com
www.Spiritual-Journey.com

This book will inform the reader about personal experiences related to a spiritual search, diets, and exercise. It is based upon the direct experience and observations of the author, who is not a medical or naturopathic doctor. This book is intended to be informational and by no means considered a substitute for advice from a medical or health professional, who should be consulted regarding any health-related issue.

The author and publisher expressly disclaim responsibility for any adverse effects arising from the use or application of the information in this book.

Gurumayi and Siddha Yoga are registered trademarks of the Siddha Foundation.

ISBN 0-9725108-0-X

Contents

Preface 5
Foreword 7
Acknowledgments 9

PART ONE

CHAPTER ONE 13
The Second Spiritual Awakening
March 1991–1993

CHAPTER TWO 21
My Early Memories
1954–1978

CHAPTER THREE 33
The First Spiritual Awakening
1978–1981

CHAPTER FOUR 41
The Third and Fourth Spiritual Awakenings
1999–2001

CHAPTER FIVE 51
The World Trade Center
September 10, 2001

PART TWO

Observations   69

Affirmations   125

Glossary of Terms   127

Next Steps   129

Conversations with a Friend   131

Addendum: Counseling Services   145

Index   147

PREFACE

THIS BOOK IS A PERSONAL JOURNEY THROUGH FORTY-SIX YEARS OF LIFE, nearly a half a century of attempting to answer the question: "Who am I?" I hope that some of the passages in this book awaken your memory and contribute to your own unfolding. Because we all are in the process of *remembering who we are.*

Trials, tribulations, suffering, pain, and ultimate joy always result in finding you're highest good, what is perfect for you in every way. So trusting in the process is essential.

The goal of this book is to bring happiness and joy into your life by involving you in a dynamically creative process. You are the chief engineer of your life; you govern your real-life experiences, each and every one of them. The second part of the book is a series of observations that help you understand that the process is ongoing for everyone. The third section is a series of real-life questions from other seekers and answers discovered while working on this book. Finally, the last section is a series of affirmations that will assist you in your own unfolding.

This writing is nondenominational and will benefit any spiritual seeker. References are made to Jesus Christ, Buddhism, ancient yogic texts, and the Bible.

In the text of this book, you will sometimes see an infinity symbol ∞. This follows key concepts and encourages you to take a few moments to dwell on the words and ideas. In addition, the book can be scanned looking for the symbol and reviewing these areas both before and after reading.

Enjoy the Journey!

We are all "Masters in the Making."

Please feel free to write of your experiences.

When I initially started this work in 1999, I saw my life as a series of separate and distinct events with intermittent spiritual occurrences—or spiritual moments, if you will. I saw my life as falling into distinct categories: husband, father, brother, son, friend, technician, writer, photographer, teacher, and spiritual seeker. By early 2001, my understanding and perceptions of spiritual events in life expanded to encompass everything. Quite contrary to the Western supposition that spiritual lifestyles are bland, deprived, and miserable, I found just the opposite to be true. Life unfolded and expanded into a richer and more abundantly satisfying experience in each and every way. In the process of unfolding my own truth, nothing was left the same; everything improved—even something as mundane as my balance on a razor (scooter) was improved.

A natural evolution occurred from being a human being having a spiritual experience, to a spiritual being having a human experience.

For this I am most grateful.

With light and love, I welcome you.

FOREWORD

IN ANY UNDERTAKING, QUESTIONS FLOW THROUGH US ALMOST INCESSANTLY: How do I start? Will I have the necessary commitment? How will I know if I'm progressing or even done?

I can tell you from the heart that <u>where you are right now is exactly where you need to be. Everything in the universe is as it should be, right now</u>.

<u>Our joys and sorrows are to teach us</u>. This life is so much broader and deeper than most of us can conceive possible.

Use this tool as a means to liberation:

- Read the book in the early morning and late evening. Make it the first and last thing you attend to each day. It will have a calming and purifying effect on you, your thoughts, and emotions.

- During the day, reflect upon some of what you recently read. Look for its relevance in your daily life.

- Give yourself enough time to notice a difference. You should start to feel lighter and easier about life. Remember to be patient; you have been the way you are for a long time. The changes come initially evolutionary, then at some point, as you are ready, they become revolutionary.

- Spend more time reflecting on topics that immediately precede the infinity symbols throughout the text, as these are key concepts.

- Share your experiences with people closest to you.

- Lastly, follow up on the "Next Steps" as noted in the back of the book.

ACKNOWLEDGMENTS

HEART FELT LOVE AND DEEPEST THANKS GO TO: Jean, my dear wife; my children; Anthony, my father; Audrey, my mother; my brother and half-brothers, stepmothers, mother-in-law, and brother-in-law; Aunt Donna; Aunt Rae; the late Uncle Ralph; Aunt Mary; and the late Uncle Daniel; my cousins, relatives, friends, and teachers.

All of you have helped bring out the Oneness in me.

Thank you to Bobby John, a psychic friend who saw this book in the ether years before it took on form.

Special gratitude goes to Belinda J. Womack and Gurumayi Chivalasananda.

*What lies behind us and what lies before us
are tiny matters compared to what lies within us.*

—RALPH WALDO EMERSON

PART ONE

CHAPTER ONE

The Second Spiritual Awakening

March 1991–1993

WHILE ON VACATION, I CAME ACROSS A BOOK WRITTEN BY THE LATE, RENOWNED IRISH PSYCHIC EDGAR CAYCE. The complete life works of the man dubbed "The Sleeping Prophet" by writer Jess Stearn was an unusual find in a little Bahamian store that sold a mix of merchandise. I was mysteriously drawn to *Edgar Cayce: Modern Prophet* (just as I had been attracted to my first yoga book in 1978). I bought it and began to read. What followed was one of the most blessed experiences of my life.

At first, I was drawn to the book to learn as much as possible about Jesus. Cayce's book was richly sprinkled with both biblical stories and personal references to the Master. Scanning the book for text referencing Jesus and especially for quotes about what "Jesus said" brought me a deeper level of understanding. I read the book in the early morning and at night prior to sleeping for approximately one-half to two hours per day. For many of us, these times during the day are especially potent in that the last thing the mind is exposed to at night remains in the subconscious the entire night. In addition, in the early morning hours, the subconscious is more open to reflection—it is rested from the night and the conscious mind has yet to start barking out new orders for the day.

During this regimen of reading and studying, I had a spiritual experience that I can only term as "an awakening." It occurred one Monday morning in March after a heavy, wet northeastern snowfall. I was walking to work and suddenly became enchanted by the virginal snowy landscape. It was a breathtaking picture, as if Claude Monet had been painting all night with a restricted palette of whites. While walking through this beautiful white picture postcard, I began spontaneously praying. Within a few moments, an overwhelming feeling that Jesus Christ was real washed over me.

I experienced profound peace, tranquility, faith, and deep feelings that Jesus was and is alive. The initial moments were the most complete and fulfilling lifetime moments in every way. I believe that the profound peace that I felt was one of Jesus' many blessings to humanity: "Peace I leave with you, my peace I give unto you: not as the world gives, give I unto you. Let not your heart be troubled, neither let it be afraid" (John 14: 27).

I also felt a deep union with all. There was a beautiful sense of Oneness flowing within me along with a distinct absence of the "small me." It filled me completely and gloriously. Time ceased to exist as I was surrounded by, and surrendered to, eternity. An engulfing rapture of a much larger definition of me occurred. A reality unfolded that had been hidden inside me by ceaseless thoughts and painful feelings; these barriers that had once seemed so important melted away. Now life existed in a beautifully panoramic pure and seemingly endless dream. In this state, awareness expanded to three hundred-sixty degrees around me, as if I could see in all directions simultaneously. As the ancient yogi masters have said, "Everything will appear when it's time" or "The Guru will appear when the disciple is ready."

With the experience came a complete absence of all fear. In fact, part of the walk was along a busily traveled road, and yet I felt no danger. A calm and confidence radiated from within me as well as the knowledge that everything would be just fine.

I realized I was willing to face the greatest fear of all—the fear of death—in the name of Jesus. I believed in Jesus and, even if it meant my life would be threatened, I would not deny my Lord.

These blessed feelings lasted for five days, slowly leaving a little each day, much to my dismay.

Unlocking the Door to Oneness
What prompted this experience? I attribute it partly to my lifestyle. At the time, I was a practicing vegetarian. (For me, spiritual awakenings have followed a pattern that I now recognize and will be further referenced in the Observations section of this book.) But I believe an even greater factor in this case was Edgar Cayce's book. Through my readings from Cayce's book, specifically regarding Jesus, I had touched upon one of the many keys to connecting to the Infinite One.

By asking, I had received an experience connecting me consciously to Jesus. I had followed an ancient promise,

"Ask and you shall receive, seek and you shall find, knock and it will be opened to you. For everyone who asks shall receive, and everyone who seeks will find and to him that knocks it shall be opened" (Luke 11: 9–10).

This truly miraculous experience washed away some of my biggest personal fears. The fear of abandonment (by God) and the fear of my own mortality were no longer part of my conscious mind. I now possessed the deep knowledge that Jesus was and is real and that His promises and blessings are true, for all people.

How can I describe this feeling of Oneness? Beauty, completeness, glory, wonder, rapture. I realized that this feeling of Oneness—the only thing truly worth effort in life—is always within us and available just for the asking. My first complete experience of Oneness unfolded quite unexpectedly and naturally. The beauty in nature coupled with prayer and a pure mind and heart unlocked the door in an instant. That door is inside you, too, and it is the portal to your own eternity.

In the Bible, Jesus said, "Wisdom is the principal thing; therefore get wisdom: and with all thy getting get understanding" (Prov. 4: 7).

What he means is that searching for understanding is more important than acquiring mere things in the physical realm. Life is so much richer than most of us dare to imagine.

The experience that we are all avidly searching for is right before us in all its glory. It is all around us always. The majority of us vainly attempt to fill the empty feeling in our hearts and lives through external means, but expensive toys won't get us back to that place which we deeply and intuitively know.

We have in varying degrees all tried a plethora of popular external methods to fulfill the deep void in our lives. What have you discovered in this search? Have you observed a pattern of reaching a plateau, a peak experience, only to háve it be followed by a period of boredom or disinterest? This is true of everything except spirituality; it is the only limitless resource to fill and continue to fill you in every way eternally. The irony is that the experience that we are searching for cannot be externally satisfied no matter what method we use. Eternal satisfaction can only come from within.

You Are the Problem—And the Answer

I have found three things to be true: We are all searching for the same thing, it cannot be found through external means, and that which we seek is already within us. So what keeps us all from eternal bliss? The individual is both the obstacle and the only one who can ultimately bring the experience unto oneself.

The obstacle that keeps us from Oneness is the ego and the stream of nonconscious thoughts so many of us have come to believe defines us. (We will discuss the ego and nonconscious thoughts in greater detail later in the book.)

The ego is a fearful child. It fears loss and change, suffering and pain. It will trade anything for short-term relief. But that is all it is: a short-term respite and not an eternal answer. Most of us through our outward search are just looking for a slightly roomier prison with nicer linens.

If we are all searching for the same thing, then we are not alone. There are many guides and helpers on the way. In fact, everyone you meet in life is part of your journey back to Oneness. You just need to pay attention to each encounter—maybe you are to help or be helped.

Random events are not truly haphazard at all. There exists a symmetry and profound order in our world. Exchanges occur on a much broader level than our normal awareness can acknowledge. Each entity is vibrating at its own frequency with its own unique set of experiences that occasionally change vibration level accordingly. A recent example of the flow in everything for me occurred while I was riding on a train and met a person in the publishing business. This superficially random event turned out to be a great help in the publishing process. Several days after meeting this person, I had some more questions about the publishing industry but was unable to reach her. Then one day as I entered the station stop and exited the train car, I saw her right in front of me.

Don't Be Afraid of Change

One of the fears we all harbor is that of change, and this type of change is no exception. We fear that opening to spirituality will cause us to become mindless, unemotional drones, which is totally incorrect. In fact, many of us already live drone-like existences concocted by modern advertising, television, and ego.

The process of evolving leads to change in perception that in turn leads you to all the other changes in your life—perhaps changes that you have long been seeking but never quite got started.

It's as if you are playing a game of hide and seek with your true self. Whenever we live out of the ego and unconscious mind, we are hiding. When we begin to change our perception and seek true Oneness, the darkness that clouds our understanding and consciousness slowly evaporates like a cloud being pierced by the sun's rays.

∞

Every aspect of life is enhanced—emotional, mental, physical, and spiritual. Relationships are purer, less turbulent, and more open. Understanding of another person's situation in life is heightened, not reduced. Every experience that you normally enjoy is enhanced, and those occasional situations you don't care for glide by effortlessly. Life begins to flow with a simplicity and grace not previously considered possible by the conscious mind that considers "Oneness" its own death. The only way to experience this bliss is to unwind the artificial character you have built up through your lifetime using the unconscious mind and ego.

My initial perceptions regarding the feeling of walking with Jesus after a beautiful snowfall were only the recognition of the removal of fear. It took many years, as the ego and unconscious mind unwound, to reach deeper feelings of Oneness. The experience was completely stored in its entirety. Wherever you find your self, start now in expanding your consciousness. The benefits will become apparent, and you will not wish to return to the "bad dream" of an ego-controlled life.

While writing this book, this awakening experience has served as a cornerstone of support. The frequent references to this chapter recharged energies and gave me the resolve to bring this book into the light.

In November of 1993, the birth of our first child occurred. Staring at him, after his troubled birth, I had the overwhelming sense that all of life—all the trials, troubles, and tribulations—had been leading up to this incredible moment. I held my son Nicholas and, for the first time in my life, cried tears of joy.

In May 1997, we were blessed again by the birth of our second child, Daniel. Once again, tears of joy streamed down my face while holding the helpless new born.

I was a different man than I was so many years ago thumbing through a book that seemed to call to me from the shelves of a small shop in the Bahamas.

CHAPTER TWO

My Early Memories

1954–1978

I WAS BORN IN THE MIDST OF A RECORD HEAT WAVE IN THE SUMMER OF 1954 ON JULY 29 IN NEW YORK CITY. We lived in a small apartment in a federal housing project in the North Bronx. When my father received a raise and notified the agency that evaluated earnings relative to rent rates (as he was required to do), he was called into a meeting and told that the thirty-six-dollar-per-month rent would be raised to fifty-two dollars per month. In addition, he was assessed a fine for failure to report a change of income of seventy-five dollars.

Our financially strapped family decided to move to Upstate New York in the Catskill Mountains. Dad took a low-paying job, and my parents started to settle into their new way of life. We were living with relatives at the time, and they reported to my father that my mother had been crying during the day. After discussions, my mother went to visit a psychiatrist in New York City. The result of the meeting was a decision to move back to New York. My mother was lonely and missed her old home.

The move back to New York was not enough to stem my mother's pain, depression, and confusion. On February 24, 1955, my mother committed suicide by jumping off a roof in Mt. Vernon, New York. She was twenty-nine years old. I was six months old at the time.

Who knows when memories are first imprinted? Some of us can hardly remember what happened yesterday, while others maintain they have crisp memories from their days in the crib. I know my mother's death made an impact on me as an infant. Years later my father spoke of a difficult birthing process and how I had to remain in the hospital several days after birth due to low birth weight. I believe I stored away the pain from those early turbulent months of my life and the loss of my mother—and later in life it edged to the surface. The season of winter, cold and barren, came to trigger emotional depressions and the perception that it's not safe to feel because feeling hurts. I now recognize that my emotions are very much tied to the seasons of the northeastern United States.

In a failed attempt to remain anonymous, my mother had cut all the labels out of her clothing—as if that could so easily erase her presence from our lives. Poor dear Father was completely crushed, and as part of passing through this extremely painful experience, he had a bleeding rectum, resulting from the loss. Tony, my older brother, suffered as well. He was just about to turn five when our mother died. One of his early memories was of our mom teaching him to pray, kneeling at his bedside. Years later, my father told me that he had never met a more religious person than my mother.

Naturally, the source of all of my memories of my

mother and her beauty are photographs. The photos of my mother recall her physical beauty and poise, never hinting at the turbulence within, the thoughts and emotions that tortured her.

My deep emotional pain, incurred at a subconscious level at six months old, would erupt forty-five years later in a final acceptance of this pain and an explosive spiritual awakening. The release of emotional pain was exhibited in physical discomfort. At various times while writing this book, tears flowed involuntarily, and I experienced a stabbing pain in the lower left abdomen, just below the navel. Eastern religions recognize that the region below the navel is the second energy field (chakra) within the body and the seat of the soul. The left side is our emotional side and the right the intellect. The emotions parallel the heart of God's divine love and the intellect that of God's divine light.

My mother's death temporarily splintered the family. My brother Tony was sent to live with our maternal Aunt Eleanor and Uncle Vincent in Long Island, New York. I was bundled away to Upstate New York in the Catskill region to live with my dear Aunt Rae and Uncle Ralph. This was a place we would call "the farm," which was in stark contrast to our New York City apartment. The farm was a place we would return to summer after summer for our family vacation. At almost one year old, I can recall the daunting task of climbing down the stairs to the first floor. I remember looking down from the top of the stairs and being afraid and then figuring out that I could safely navigate the trip backwards. The experience of being afraid and navigating backwards is part of what is helping write this account of my own evolution, in this incarnation.

As the center of my world emotionally was rocked to the core in early life, I would learn to live and figure out what happened in retrospect, until mastering enough of my own emotions to consciously create.

Father remarried prior to my second birthday, and the family was reunited. We formed a home in a three-bedroom apartment (eventually six of us) on the third floor of a five-story walk-up building. The apartment building was at the top of the first hill on Clay Avenue, located at 160th Street in the Bronx. It was the only white brick building on the long street.

My preschool years were mostly quiet and uneventful. However, it was during those early childhood years that I first perceived a definite difference between the way my stepmother acted toward me and the way my father treated me. Dad was softer, warmer, and more caring. My stepmother Margaret was crisper, colder, and more of a routine caretaker. Again, a small pain ripples through my left lower abdominal area as I remember my stepmother. My father's second marriage resulted in two half-brothers. Since my preschool years were spent mostly playing by myself and imagining, I welcomed the playmates.

Trying Telepathy
One of my earliest conscious memories was the juncture point in communications where I could understand what was being said, but did not have the muscular control to reply verbally. One particular day, as my father and stepmother were speaking, in frustration and unable to communicate I wondered to my father, "Why don't we just think it?" I even directed thoughts to them in hopes that they would "hear" me and respond, but they did not reply.

My second attempt was an even stronger message: "Why don't we think it, like we used to?" At a little more than one-and-a-half years old, I had attempted to communicate telepathically. Was this the way I was used to communicating, perhaps in another incarnation? Later in school, I experienced similar moments of "knowingness," times when I seemed to touch some universal truth inside of me—my true self, not the destructive ego that would later nearly take my life.

On the first day of first grade, Hurricane Donna pounded the East Coast and even knocked out step-grandma's back bedroom window. Dad put us in the car and drove us to school that day. Normally, we would walk to school. We went to Catholic school, Our Lady of Victory, on Webster Avenue in the Bronx. The complex included a school, church, convent, and rectory. I especially liked the school uniforms: dark blue dress-up pants, a light blue ironed shirt, and a dark blue tie. The gold letters "OLV" were stitched at a sixty-five-degree angle on the tie.

Reveling in the fact that I was now more like my older brother Tony, I anxiously awaited homework so that I could be just like my big brother. But each day I trudged down the long hill to home and my stepmother Margaret, who was waiting on the stoop smoking a cigarette, and expressed frustration that I did not get any homework yet. After about two weeks, we got our first homework assignment: a punishment lesson in which I had to write "I must not talk in class" twenty-five times.

The punishment was the result of a free-for-all that occurred when our substitute teacher stepped out of the classroom. The moment she left the room, the room erupted into pandemonium with children throwing things, hopping out of their seats, fighting, running around, and yelling. Although I was far from the perfect student, this particular occasion found me much more introspective, observing the craziness in class with hands folded and centered on the desk. The full awareness that there had to be more to life than what I could see, touch, hear, taste, and smell—otherwise, the entire thing made no sense—dawned in that moment of chaos and distraction. There was a quiet voice within me, and, even as a six-year-old, I recognized it.

I experienced another psychic moment in first grade. It was late on a Friday afternoon in the spring, after I had emptied the trash for the class. Considered a perk at the time. When I reentered the room, I could feel that something was amiss. For the first time, that I remember, I could feel the energy in a given area and determine if it were positive or otherwise. And this energy was definitely not positive. The teacher asked me why my little plaid briefcase was empty. I told her that I had finished all my homework already. Instead of expanding my interests further or giving me a special assignment, she scolded me: homework is for home, not school, she said. Promptly she went down the hall to inform my step-aunt of my crime, requesting that she relay this information to my stepmother.

Life with Stepmother

The neighborhood in the Bronx where I lived and went to school offered a bleak color scheme, mostly red brick, concrete, and asphalt. Occasionally, I would notice spring and how beautiful the few trees on our street were, but for the most part, it was an uninspiring place. As was life with my stepmother Margaret. Again and again, my stepmother put me down. Through the years, I grew used to that feeling of self being crushed.

Please note that I love my stepmother, especially for the role that she played in my development, which was essential. I forgive her completely; she did her best and she had a difficult path herself. She was the oldest daughter of an Irish family, growing up in the Bronx with her three sisters. At the age five, she suffered an accident that left her left leg scarred for life. In the 1930s, milk was often delivered in metal containers. She was reaching for the milk on the kitchen table, when the container fell and severely injured her leg. The injury required numerous stitches, visible all the way up the front of her shin. The leg never grew properly after that; it was visibly smaller than the other one. Her shoe size was different, so whenever she bought shoes she needed two pairs.

Her father fell off a scaffold and died when she was twenty years old. Margaret immediately stepped into the role of breadwinner for her mom and three sisters. After she met my father, had a whirlwind courtship, and fell in love for the first time in her life, the honeymoon ended abruptly. Upon arriving home from the Niagara Falls honeymoon, she found herself with an instant family: a six-year-old and a one-and-a-half-year-old. Suddenly, she was the caretaker of two children, who were not her own. It takes a special person to be able to accept this situation. I believe she felt as if she came second to my brother and me in the family. In the next few years, she had two children of her own, ten months apart.

Finances were tight in our rapidly expanding family. Margaret's life became an endless loop of cooking, cleaning, sewing, and taking care of four children. There was little personal satisfaction in her life. Margaret started drinking, at some point, and continued to smoke cigarettes, neglecting her health. She had little to wear; her clothes often were handed down from family members. She neglected her feet so badly, that the calluses on the back of her heels were a good half-inch thick, with dead skin peeling off.

Around the summer of 1967, she was attacked in the front of our building by a women three or four times her weight. The altercation left her with a terrible black eye and crushed self-esteem. The conflict centered on the neighbor's child and my younger brother. During the fight, my brother almost got his eye poked out with a spiked piece of wrought iron. I remember her complaining to my father that he wouldn't even buy a piece of steak to put on the eye. I wasn't there for most of it, but when I arrived, I thought that she was bleeding; in reality, she had relieved her bladder.

Margaret's only source of enjoyment, aside from her own children, was her mother and sisters, who lived above us for quite sometime. However, once our family moved to Upstate New York, she was completely cut off. Our budget didn't stretch to many long-distance calls. Finances were so tight, that we almost lost the house at one point. My father was rear-ended in a car accident, which later provided the family with a settlement of some seven or eight hundred dollars. That money was needed to keep the family afloat. Margaret did an amazing job managing the family's finances, based upon the little that we had. She neglected her dental health, because the family did not have the money for such expenses. She put herself and her needs last, but then resented it deeply. My father worked two jobs most of his work life to help make ends meet.

Moving to Middletown

At some point in my turbulent high school years or early college days, I remember thinking, incorrectly at that time, that thoughts were not controllable and that being alive meant that I had to suffer from an endless stream of painful thoughts and painful feelings without peace.

If only I had known then what I know now: that we have complete control over every single thought that passes through our consciousness. We create the thought, and then reap the reward or punishment of it.

The thoughts I created in my high school years were full of pain and anger. Shortly before I entered high school, my father decided to move the family to a town called Middletown in Upstate New York. The timing of the move was propitious. I had not been accepted into any of the Catholic high schools to which I had applied because of poor test scores. I don't know why I was shocked. I had a prophetic dream about opening the mailed test results and doing poorly on the high school entrance exam. While taking the test at Fordham University, I mistakenly coded the answers vertically, instead of horizontally, across the answer sheet. Realizing the error very late and panicking, I attempted unsuccessfully to retake the four-hour test in a half-hour after first erasing the original answers. Clearly discussing this with the proctor would have been the better approach.

As they had always been, finances were tight after our move to Middletown. Isolated from her mother and sisters who remained now in Yonkers, New York, Margaret accelerated her self-destructive behavior of drinking and smoking. I believe she had a genetic disposition to alcohol and was quite depressed for most of her adult life. Her own family eventually moved to Middletown years later. By then, it was already far too late to help her; Margaret had been diagnosed with advanced throat cancer.

While it was clear that the love between my father and Margaret was long lost, they did not fight much. My relationship with Margaret, on the other hand, had become difficult, combative, even violent. I am not pleased to admit that during several stormy screaming matches, I struck her. Living with her drunken screaming and spitting became too much on some days. It would hurt my father, but it was crushing me, so I fought back with whatever I could.

While some days I can only think of the painful times, there were also happy moments in my teen years: I got a part-time job and bought a car that gave me a degree of independence. I developed an interest in psychic subjects and a belief in psychic phenomenon. I read and dreamed of other realms beyond this physical plane. A neighbor loaned me a book about an Indian saint, Sathya Sai Baba, that opened up other possibilities on this physical plane. I also had a soft, sweet, beautiful girlfriend. I was seventeen and in love for the first time. She brought rays of sunshine into my life through high school and part of college.

While in college, my girlfriend felt that my interest in computers threatened us as a couple. She complained that we were growing apart, but I was interested in acquiring skills so that I could provide a living. We broke up in my third semester of college, hurting me deeply, but nothing compared to a future depression.

And so the seeds of pain were sown—planted by my mother's early death and being ripped away from my father and brother for a good part of the first year of my life—and nurtured by my stepmother's emotional abuse. It is my sincere belief that I never heard my stepmother say, "I love you." I did not sense just how deep these pains were and how long it would take to resolve them.

As I completed college and became a part of the workforce, I locked in on other reality belief systems to cope with the pain of life and to feed my quiet longing and refusal to believe that pain was all there is to life.

CHAPTER THREE

The First Spiritual Awakening

1978–1981

IN THE SPRING OF 1978, I WENT THROUGH MY FIRST SPIRITUAL AWAKENING WITHOUT KNOWING WHAT WAS OCCURRING. I was working as a computer consultant in Philadelphia at the time, and I shared a weekend house in Fort Lee, New Jersey. I took a course at a local school to learn how to meditate. The process of spiritual awakening through meditation was like a beautiful spring day with just the right amount of warmth, freshness in the air, beauty, purity, and portends of better things to come. As I write this, I now realize that this awakening paralleled the seasons in that year.

As I indicated earlier, my emotional state rode a seasonal roller coaster. Down periods were locked into winter, mirroring the bleakest time in nature and within my own internal biological clock. When I was an infant, my world was turned upside down by my mother's suicide, which occurred in winter. In the preceding winter, I had gone through a ripple of the blues, missing the environment that I was familiar with, and feeling empty inside the stark, cold city environment. Spring always brought newness and hope, summer contained deep warmth, fall indicated a change was coming, and ultimately the next winter would result in a deep emotional crash.

I had a great many mystical, wonderful, and magical experiences within the meditation process. On the first day of meditation class during a lunch break, I had the experience of moving a plant by placing my hand in its energy field. While discussing the class with a friend, I subtly placed my hand in the plant's energy field, without touching it. The restaurant had no direct sunlight or lighting changes during our short lunch. As the meal continued, a small miracle occurred in front of us, the philodendron plant moved distinctly toward me. Throughout lunch, I stayed seated at the table. I believe the plant detected the warmth and love pulsing from my soul and moved closer to me as an interpretation of light and warmth.

During this time, in the 1970s, I had several psychic experiences. I found that I could "see" the outcome of the roll of backgammon dice in advance of rolling them. I saw a negative image of the dice as if viewing a piece of negative film.

I also got mental images, once again resembling a negative of film, of the contents of my mailbox. I was able to "see into" my mailbox from fifty feet away. Sure enough, when I opened the keyed little door, the number of letters and their position inside the box was exactly as I had seen in my mental image.

I was intrigued by this other world that seemed to be opening for me. I wanted to see more of it. I stuck to a survival diet of fruit and nuts, eating for spiritual purity. I expanded my yoga practice daily.

Masters in the Making

We are all "Masters in the Making" or works in progress, evolving through the eons. We are born, grow, experience, and evolve in a process of returning to God. In my life, I have been blessed by this awareness, the pain of a quiet longing that has never been satisfied by anything other than God's love. I can truly say that I feel complete and the pain is gone. I have just experienced a kundalini energy wave from the lower spine to the brain, originating from the heart. In order to survive the emotional pains of my early life, I started living from the mind, shunning and shutting off emotions for most of my life. Many of us do this without awareness.

During this time, I had some wonderful meditative experiences.

In a deep meditative state, I asked my first question: "What is life?" An awareness echoed back, "Evolution." I essentially had asked the primordial question of "Who am I?" in relationship to life and what is my purpose. We as a race are all on a spiritual evolutionary path as that's all there ultimately is.

∞

Everything on this planet is a tool for learning and teaching. We are born, grow, learn, and die. The answer, "Evolution," flowed through every layer of my existence and rang with a truth that I had not known existed. Someone, some force, was actually "out there" listening to me, little insignificant me, wow! Actually, later in life, I found that there is something inside which reflects and projects our outside experience.

As I write this, a kundalini energy wave has traversed from the top of my head to my feet. The universe's answer to "What is life?" was a beautiful feeling and profound knowledge added to my expanding psychic awareness. Recently, if I speak or think a truth, a wave of energy is felt though my body on the right side. If I feel a truth, a similar wave is felt on the left side.

The Power of Thought and Energy

In conjunction with this time, my favorite uncle was having cancer removed from his brain. Uncle Ralph was the physically strongest person I ever knew. At one time in his life, he actually lifted the back of an old Ford, so that his father-in-law could replace the flat tire. My father would often say that when Uncle Ralph grabbed your arm, it was like a vice grip. Uncle Ralph also possessed a powerful memory; he could easily card count in most card games. He had made a living in his youth playing cards in the back of a little candy store, sometimes playing for more than ten hours in a day. Uncle Ralph had back-to-back brain surgeries: an eighteen-hour procedure followed by a twenty-one-hour operation. I wanted to help and went into a meditative state and asked the question, "What does he need?" The awareness replied, "Energy."

So I sent him energy. At some point, either in a dream or in meditation, I had the awareness of two energy fields meeting (there was a visual buzz surrounding two distinct entities, like a cartoon picture when the character touches an electric cord). After this, a discharge occurred, and I awoke the next day feeling completely recharged, refreshed, rejuvenated, and feeling good about my beloved uncle. Uncle Ralph recuperated and survived an additional ten years after these operations.

Make It What You Will
During this time, I also was struggling with the concept of cause and effect or how things happened in life. Once again, I turned to meditation. However, before I could even verbalize the question, an answer formed inside of me: "Make it what you will." Ah, I feel another beautiful wave of kundalini energy, bliss, and love.

∞

"Make it what you will" is another profound reverberation from the cosmos. Not only is there a profound force in the universe, it even understands what you are attempting to ask. This Consciousness works in every language, every culture, and every person simultaneously.

These two pieces of information are universal truths, not unique to any individual, and provide a concrete foundation toward your own liberation. We are all attempting to evolve, and we do make our life what it is, through a trilogy of thoughts, feelings, and actions.

Love Is No Match for the Ego
During this time, I fell intensely and intimately in love with a truly wonderful woman. This relationship was deeper emotionally than any I had had before. I felt at one with her, complete, in her embrace.

We had a beautiful time together, including a brief holiday in the Blue Ridge Mountains in Virginia. The tranquility and beauty were wonderful. One morning while jogging I had the experience of hearing an eagle's wings while it veered off in a direction, with a whoosh, whoosh, whoosh sound. Shortly after this, I thought it would be nice to see some deer. Around the next bend, there were three deer in a small group eating some morning grass by the roadside. I was quite in tune with nature at this time in my life.

Even though my personal life was going well and my spiritual life was growing richer every day, I still could not escape my negative thoughts. Eventually, my ego sabotaged our relationship. I failed to control my negative thoughts and, during the later stage of our relationship, became difficult to deal with. I did not understand how powerful the ego was and that the strength of the spirit could magnify its poisonous power. Between 1975 and 1978, I totaled two automobiles. The accidents paralleled my emotional and spiritual crashes. Each accident involved no other vehicles: in the first crash, I fell asleep at sixty-five miles per hour, and in the second, I had a few too many drinks.

I ultimately had a clinical depression and moved from Philadelphia back to a new apartment in New York City. I then returned back to my dad's house in Middletown, New York. I withdrew from life, and it rapidly withdrew from me. I was now living dangerously close to my mother's mental and emotional distress, which ultimately ended her life here on earth. The utter despair was crushing. I was stuck in my own negative thoughts, unable to escape from the black hole of pain that I had created. The pain was so acute that my bones hurt; my left elbow ached with the amount of energy that I had turned against myself. My hair started to turn gray (which actually started slowly at age twenty).

I began to pray to God and Sathya Sai Baba in desperate

hopes for some relief. I went into a hospital. The doctors tried numerous types of medicine, but nothing worked. The environment I was in was more like a sterile prison then that of a healing place for emotionally sick people. The setting was completely offensive to anyone with feelings. One night, I ran away, racing more than five miles down the road. I desperately wanted to escape the terrible feelings inside of me.

A few days later, I checked myself out of the hospital against medical advice. I lasted a week or two outside and wound up back in another hospital that provided a much better setting. The significance of the environment was key to my recovery, and I thanked my sister-in-law for the recommendation. Here I reintroduced yoga into my daily regimen, and that greatly speeded up my healing process. Eventually, I grew better and was released from the hospital. This experience was so painful that I did not meditate for almost five years after my initial exposure. I had grown to fear the very tool that would eventually aid in liberation.

Falling Again

I had pulled myself, with help, out of the first major emotional abyss of my lifetime. However, I had set myself up for another fall by 1980. This time, no love was needed to destroy my life. I could now accomplish this without any assistance. In reflecting, the pain and suffering all through my life from birth to early childhood and through the teenage years had now come full circle as anger turned inward. I was angry with God for my place on this physical plane. Angry at the pain and suffering, angry at the enormously difficult times that I had, simultaneously somehow knowing that there was more to me than these problems. Something good, loving, and powerful would eventually unfold, I told myself, if I could survive the rough spots.

My father and brother helped me survive the late 1970s and early 1980s. They, as well as my dad's third wife Dottie, provided pillars of strength. I remembered, in the heat of shouting matches, my stepmother used to cruelly tell me that I was crazy like my mother. I feared her taunts were becoming reality. I had begun to contemplate suicide.

As I write these words, I feel pain in my lower left side, more tears to come, more pain to be released. I was now two-thirds of the way to my own destruction. To stop the emotional pain, thought, and word, the only missing puzzle piece was deed.

I am asking God, at this very moment, to fill me with His divine love, to replace the pained feelings with pure love. After stopping briefly, my conscious mind said, "John, stop this and get on and grow up." The part of me that I have lived out of for more than forty-six years, my emotional side, says, it's okay to feel the pain, it's okay to let it out, it really happened, and you never emotionally accepted it, you just stored it in your emotional memory. Now, it is time to release the pain so that it can be replaced with God's love. Nature abhors a vacuum. I am listening much more these days to my emotional side. The conscious mind as of late has toned down its volume and intensity as if to become friends again.

CHAPTER FOUR

The Third and Fourth Spiritual Awakenings

1999–2001

DURING THIS PERIOD, I HAD AGAIN BECOME A VEGETARIAN, for a third time. I focused on purifying the body with organic foods, fruits, vegetables, plenty of water, and herbal teas. Eating a balanced vegetarian diet was necessary for me. During the day, I concentrated more and more on the spiritual aspect of life. I switched yoga teachers. I felt it was time for a change, and my former yoga teacher's approach was too Western for my tastes. This turned out to be a fortunate move. My new yoga instructor, Chaya, indirectly connected me to the Guru.

On a beautiful evening in the summer of August 1999 after yoga class, we had our regular meditation period. During this meditation, I had a beautiful vision of a dark circle in the foreground, which I equated to earth. The dark center was surrounded by a beautiful, pure, deep purple color. The purple realm is the crown chakra, the seventh energy field that surrounds the head. As I saw this beautiful purple color, a deep feeling of purity and time-lessness pervaded my conscious. The color was the purest and most brilliant color that I have ever seen. There was an absence of time. Eternity existed within this color, and a wonderful experience of blissfulness emerged. Bliss filled me completely as I intuitively knew that this was the start of a new chapter in the spiritual awakening process. A new doorway had been opened. This was a most gentle experience compared to the first dawning of enlightenment and spiritual awakening.

Meeting My Guru

The spiritual process needs to be guided by a master of this technique, someone who has been there before. In August 2000, I was blessed by meeting the Guru of the Siddha lineage, Gurumayi Chidvilasananda. The weekend, called an Intensive, encompassed spiritual stories, chanting, and meditation. I spent these two days in silence (except for chanting). The purpose of the weekend was to help participants focus on the inner experience. During the weekend stay, I went to Nitanada's temple to pray and upon leaving, tears of joy streamed uncontrollably from me. On the final day, we received the Guru's discourse, chanted with her, and received her blessings known as darshan.

I have always tried to see and feel spiritual experiences to their fullest and was completely unprepared for what followed. The Guru gave me her blessings via several touches with a peacock feather, and initially nothing "happened." However, little by little, a new blissful experience unfolded. It is said that the Guru radiates divine love like the sun radiates heat and warmth, because of the amount of love inside the Guru. Minutes after the blessing, I felt a wonderful warmth descend over me as if I had just spent hours in the summer sun at the beach. The bliss warmed me from inside out and actually flushed my face red reflecting her radiant energy.

How the Stock Market Became My Teacher

The fourth spiritual awakening unfolded quickly and culminated in a Oneness experience as well as a physical manifestation.

Like many of us, I was an investor between 2000 and 2001. My wife and I had a portfolio of stocks, which I believed I had learned to handle fairly well over the last fifteen years. After extensive research and analysis, I decided to place a sizeable portion of our investing monies into one particular stock. What unfolded was the best, worst, best, worst, and finally best experience of my life compressed over a period of one year.

In March 2000, the value of our investments soared. Naturally having been an investor for more than fifteen years, I took a long-term vision of investing. But my investment horizon time frame for this particular investment was shorter. I expected it to change everything within two to three years.

I thought I knew linearly just how my world would change. I desperately wanted my freedom from the nine-to-five world and present career that I had grown tired of after almost thirty years. The feeling that there was something else that I should be doing intensified deep inside of me. The very purpose of my life, my reason for this incarnation, was starting to dim. I needed to make some changes. We all have a sense of our gifts, and that's what the subtle feeling was echoing for me. This deep and subtle perception came from my true self, not the ego. And this stock was going to be my way to this life change.

But I was still plagued by a negativity birthed by the loss of my mother and an enormously unstable start on this planet. I was still filled with anger toward my step-mother. As my "chosen" stock tumbled and rolled from June 24, 2000, until March 28, 2001, I increasingly tied my future and emotions to the stock market.

The market first crashed between March 2000 and May 2000. During that period, emotionally I acknowledged the passing of my stepmother years earlier. The angst I was feeling over the market released a sense of loss and emotions that were bottled up for more than twenty-five years. The pain of loss, heartache, and tears of sadness flooded me. When she was fatally ill, I thought that I could not change my relationship with her. After her death, I did not shed a single tear for her. Clearly the pain felt after all those years of emotional abuse had long since crushed any attachment to her. The negative impact of my drive for freedom also unwittingly affected my dear wife during the first crash. Her sense of loss and pain was felt and mirrored the trapped pain of her parents' divorce.

I possess a single-mindedness that many times is initially painful, but ultimately the highest good and joy unfolds from it. My father had angioplasty the week the markets started to roll over in March 2000. I picked him up from the hospital to take him home that Saturday. When I briefly explained what had occurred in the stock market, he quietly told me to sell. He was put in my energy space as a messenger, but I ignored him.

My dear wife also softly whispered that we should sell,

but by now my negative side, so full of ego and greed, was in control. The first crash was over toward the end of May, and slowly the markets recovered. With the help of time, friends, family, our children, and the markets, I had mostly recovered from the first nightmarish experience.

My chosen stock reached another new high in June 2000, and I was freed of the pain. My ego remained shaken but nonetheless intact. Everyone healed quickly from the three-month mini-crash. My father was put back into my energy space a second time at our house. Of course, Dad told me to sell again. My wife also told me to sell, again quietly. The information I had said it would be significantly better by year's end, so I told her we should wait until year-end. This was in conjunction with my own plans and expectations.

The forty weeks that followed were filled with emotional ups and downs, pain of loss, depression, guilt, ego, greed, fear, gambling, and a host of addictive, compulsive, and obsessive behaviors. I swung back and forth from living in the past to living in the future, and the intensity levels were more than I had imagined possible. It wasn't until much later, and after much reflection, that I saw the significance of the forty weeks from the second market peak to bottoming out. A full-term pregnancy is forty weeks. At a subconscious level, I had engineered a rebirthing.

Still believing the misinformation that I had projected, I wanted to see this investment through, to stick with the stock until the good markets arrived at year-end. My "rebirthing" was manifested in physical pain—a deep pain in the heart, a burning torture accompanied by stabbing pain in the stomach area. I was eating dark chocolate, taking "herbal-ups," and drinking St. John's Wort tea to fend off a deeper depression. If it were not for my dear wife and a few close friends, I would have snapped under the pressure of my own self-made hell.

I had succeeded in creating my perception of heaven, followed immediately by hell, twice in a one-year period. I would wake up in the middle of the night or after a nap and think, "How could I have done this? What the hell was I thinking?" I would look at our two unsuspecting children and imagine deprivations that my stubbornness could wreak upon them. It was as if my soul's entire bad karma had rained down on me with no intent of letting up. Of course, what can appear as "bad" karma can, in reality, be "good" karma. We may need to experience pain to learn.

My wife was worried. She pointed out that I was in a bad emotional state and needed help. I began to realize that she was right. I was getting much worse. Slowly, I began paying attention to my thoughts and emotions, looking at the tremendous negativity I had created.

One morning, my absolute bottom, after missing several nights of sleep, I confided to my friend and neighbor during the morning commute. Weeping, I told him that I felt as if I were being emotionally crucified. I told him that I would prefer an actual crucifixion to my present emotional state. Again, I didn't realize what was happening. The old definition of me was dying; the material world dominated by money, ego, greed, and power was no longer my god. I would no longer serve or attempt to serve two masters. Living out of the present tense now carried with it sharp emotional and physical pains. Through this emotional death of my past, the way was being cleared for abundant miracles.

That cloudy March day, I wore sunglasses through the

morning commute to hide the involuntary tears that flowed. The depths of emotional and mental torture were numbing. The deep perception that God would not allow something this painful to occur without a wonderful result allowed me to get through it. My mother-in-law echoed my advice to her during a dark period in her life and told me to keep thinking positive. She also agreed that something wonderful would unfold once I got past the pain.

In my life, I never cried for the passing of my own mother, thinking that I didn't have any reason to, that it was a sign of weakness, and that I never really knew her. I now understand that nothing could be further from the truth. For as long as I could remember, I have had a pain in my solar plexus area, a discomfort that never left, a constant pressure. I needed to weep for my mother.

Little by little, my neighbor and I unraveled the problem, thread by thread, and figured out that things were not as bad as initially envisioned. In addition, I had started slowly replacing negative thoughts and emotions with their positive counterparts, a huge help. One by one, the thoughts and emotions were starting to transition in my favor. I started exercising again, boosting my thoughts and feelings again toward the positive.

The deep feelings of loss and helplessness still dominated my emotions, but I slowly recognized that this experience was actually an enormous gift. The gift was freeing me emotionally from a pain that I had subconsciously carried around for the last forty-five years—from the loss of my mother.

I noticed that emotional pain is trapped in all of us, layer by layer amazingly, in reverse sequence of the event. Gradually, I freed myself from living (existing) in the past and future. I became firmly and completely grounded in the now, the only time that truly exists. Tranquility replaced my addictive, compulsive, and obsessive behaviors. By no longer seeking to control everything, I had wrested control from the ego.

I relearned something known before: Our minds are receivers, not transmitters, in our life. The quiet mind of a meditative state is to make room for God to communicate to us, to answer a question, or to feel something subtle. The conscious mind focusing on the endless streams of tasks to be done blocks the connection to God, like jamming radio airwaves with diverse random frequencies.

I now understood that most of the trials and tribulations of life were continued lessons and nothing more. My focus became infinitely more spiritual than before, deeper, more committed and profound. My heart was opening from all of this, the ego was subsiding, and a clearer view of me was emerging. I now had evolved from a human with occasional glimpses of spiritual experiences when I first started this book, to a spiritual being having a human experience.

Everything, everyone, all thoughts and feelings were now spiritual. All music had a wonderful spiritually awakened quality to it. God, not earthly dramas, became the subject of love songs. The sweetness of the melodies and notes were all the more so, with God as the central figure. The voices and instruments were praising the Almighty.

Spring exploded in the Northeast with a vibrancy of color that had been hidden through winter's long sleep. In my new awareness, nature seemed more alive than ever. I no longer used sunglasses, as I truly loved seeing the light of God. Morning dew on the grass shimmered into a wonder-filled rainbow of crystal pure gems against the lush green outdoor carpet. I realized that <u>I had created every single obstacle in my life to create friction, then to resolve that friction by generating traction toward God, toward His light and love.</u>

Gratitude for all that I still had was filling in and of itself. I thanked God for the experiences of the past year in order to break through to this point.

A Dose of God's Energy

Once I had witnessed the miracle of God's divine energy after yoga and meditation on a summer evening in 1999. I experienced it again while sitting at my desk one day on the 59th floor of the World Trade Center Tower 2 building. On April 24, 2001, at approximately 3:30 P.M., the most beautiful object I have ever seen—a spherical ball shimmering and sparkling full of God's pure divine energy—appeared before me. It was three dimensional in construction and golden in color with white sparkles emitting from it. My initial reaction was that someone in the work area was playing a joke on me. However, after looking around and determining that it was unlikely that the object was a holographic practical joke, I examined it more closely.

I sat in amazement, knowing it was special, wanting to touch it, and at the same time not wanting to disturb the experience. Frozen for several minutes in awe, I watched the orb sparkle and shimmer. This crystal-like golden sphere gave off white light like a sparkler. At the time, I thought that this was a wonderful manifestation. Later, after consulting my spiritual guidebooks, I realized—the Christ-Buddha energy had arrived.

∞

Sitting at my desk, waves of kundalini energy flowed from head to toe and back. Tears of joy now well up in my eyes as I remember the experience and realize I have a much better vision of God's divine plan, not just for me, but for everyone. The purity of the dancing gold white sphere and its sparkling brilliance were inspirational and awing. A sincere love for all humanity filled me completely. I finally knew what I needed so desperately to accomplish in this lifetime. I had been blessed to infinity.

Gradually, the remaining layers of negativity peeled away, leaving purity and contentment in their place.

The knowledge and experience that the golden white light truly exists is indeed humbling. We are all part of divinity and divine in our own unique right.

Daily, the ego needs less and less, and I need it less and less.

Thank you, God!

CHAPTER FIVE

The World Trade Center

September 10, 2001

THIS MONDAY STARTED LIKE MOST, except that this day marked vacation's end and children returning to school sporting their summer tans. The weather was invitingly warm, sunny, and calm with clear blue skies and dry relative humidity.

Our oldest child's school had delayed opening due to construction expansion to accommodate the growing population of baby boomers' children in our town. Located in the Saddle River Valley of northern New Jersey about thirty miles outside of New York City, the County of Bergen was originally incorporated in the 1600s and today is a sleepy community of large properties, trees, and lawns. Many of the town's street names bear witness to the days of the Native American with names like Oratam and Lenape. Oratam was a famous chief, and Lenape was the name of a tribe who were the first settlers of the valley.

Over the weekend, I had decided to take a later train into work at the World Trade Center (WTC) Tower Two.

I wanted to participate in our family's first-day-of-school traditions—picture taking in front of the house and a hearty French toast breakfast. Ever since my son Nicholas had been introduced to solid foods, he'd loved French toast. We nicknamed it "sizzle toast" as he would frequently help me mix the batter and always marveled at the sound of the bread meeting the hot pan. He would laugh heartily as he said, "Sizzle toast."

Our younger child, Daniel, would start preschool on Tuesday, September 11, 2001.

Nicholas had the mixed feelings of excitedly looking forward to the start of grade two and at the same time missing summer and Mom.

My typical commute into the Trade Center involved a train from Allendale, New Jersey, at about 7:50 A.M., arriving in Hoboken, New Jersey, at approximately 8:40. The train for our route was diesel powered with passenger cars containing five seats across, two on one side and three on the other. This late in the morning rush hour the first train would not fill with passengers.

Upon arrival at Hoboken, I would take a short walk downstairs to connect to the Path system. The trains labeled WTC would bring me to the base of both towers, about three or four stories underground. The foundations of the buildings were eight stories below ground level. Double tracks serviced by multiple trains of ten cars each moved the volume of commuters to this destination, which for many would be the final leg of their commute.

Waves and waves of humanity would walk through the turnstiles with either a prepaid card or cash. To save time on commuting, the prepaid card was helpful. Doing a commute like this—approximately one hour to one hour and fifteen minutes each way—required some foresight and planning. A minute saved by being in the front car of the first train would start you at Hoboken a little ahead of the wave of people on your own train. This extra minute or two could allow you to catch a sooner departing train from Hoboken that often resulted in a total savings of ten minutes.

On the Path train system you rarely got to sit. Standing in a corner toward either extreme of the car was a preferred spot on the densely packed train cars. Visible floor space on the train was nonexistent.

Like many of us, I never knew how good I had it—working at the World Trade Center—until it was too late. The convenience and ease of commute to my job in the Trade Center were wonderful and seldom appreciated. There was no need for me to see the outside world once I entered my train at Allendale, New Jersey. I arrived at the WTC efficiently.

Upon arrival at the World Trade Center multiple escalators on either side of the train greeted commuters, followed by a massive second bank of ten separate escalators. Those who simply wanted to ride the escalator stood to the right, leaving those in a rush to walk up the climbing stairs on the left.

After a multiple-story escalator ride, commuters would arrive at the base of the towers at the concourse level. Literally, the whole world passed through our doors daily. During the summertime, I remember the droves of tourists with children in tow gawking at the facility, which we called our workplace. The Trade Center was a community all by itself housing retail stores, banks, brokerage offices, a twenty-story hotel, and no fewer than thirty eating establishments. Charles Schwab, Citicorp, and Chase Manhattan (now J.P. Morgan Chase) had multiple locations with automated teller machines. The World Financial Center (WFC) was connected to the complex via a pedestrian walkway at the Hudson River level facing New Jersey.

The retail space in the WTC was the equivalent to several large-scale malls combined. There was a three-story Borders bookstore, a Godiva chocolatier store, Banana Republic, J. Crew, Gap clothing stores, Radio Shack, a music store, toy stores, a florist, a pharmacy, several candy/newsstand stores, and several jewelry stores to name a few.

In the summer, the outside concourse frequently hosted multiple daily concerts featuring jazz, pop, and country and western. The site occupied sixteen acres of the most developed land in North America housing more than fifty thousand workers per day in the largest office complex on the planet. The property was originally owned by the Port Authority of New York and New Jersey but was sold to a private firm, just six weeks before the September 11 attack. Many nationalities would converge in this facility to tour and work. It was originally designed to last for ten thousand years.

The vitality of the World Trade Center area was dwarfing, bringing together the A, E, C, 1, 2, 3, N, R, and Path trains connecting to the Bronx, Queens, Brooklyn, upper Manhattan, and New Jersey. Many of these trains would arrive or pass through the area every ten minutes during rush hour. Further out commuters from Connecticut, Westchester, Upstate New York, and Long Island added to the daily stream of humanity. In addition, a ferry system traversed the Hudson River to bring additional commuters.

The top of the World Trade Center's observation deck, located in Tower One, would open at 9:30 A.M. On most clear days, lines of visitors would start to form by 9:15 A.M. as the view around the area was unparalleled.

Once I arrived at the base of WTC Tower Two, after walking about three city blocks indoors, I would take an elevator from the first floor directly to the forty-fourth floor. The elevator was so large that it had doors on each side, so as not to necessitate turning around after initially loading. There was a bank of six of these elevators carrying as many as fifty people during rush hours.

I worked in Tower Two. The friendly security guards greeting us daily along with the policemen stationed there added to our sense of security. I softly remarked to one of the young officers, "You know you're getting older when the policemen look so young." He just smiled. The officer had a baby face and was probably no older than twenty-five. Sadly, I don't know if he survived the events of September 11, 2001.

When I took the position back in October 2000, I remembered thinking vaguely, "Oh, wasn't this the place that they tried to bomb?" Being an optimist, I quickly reassured myself, "They tried that already and didn't succeed."

September 11, 2001

On that fateful day, due to the grace of God, I did not follow my normal routine, which would have me arriving at Tower Two about 8:50 A.M. As I had done the day before, I decided to take a slightly later train so that I could make breakfast for the boys, take some more pictures of them getting ready for school, and seeing them off on their new adventure.

At 8:50 A.M., I was on a late train about two miles outside of the Hoboken rail yard.

Suddenly there was a commotion, and people turned to look out the southwest view window toward Tower One. I could see cigarette-like smoke billowing slowly out of Tower One. Someone on the train with a radio said that a small plane had hit the tower.

My first thought was: terrorists. With the Hudson River only a few thousand feet from the Trade Center area, I reasoned that no sane pilot would choose to strike the towers. A pilot facing desperate circumstances would do everything possible to survive and protect those in the towers, probably using the river as an emergency landing field.

I never made it to the New York side that day.

Upon arriving in Hoboken, the Path system's public address indicated that there was no service to the WTC stop; however, service to Thirty-third Street continued. I figured that they would close the towers today. So I decided to return home and telecommute. While waiting for the 9:35 train to take me home, a person ran up to me in a crazed manner and said a second plane had hit Tower Two and erupted into a ball of flames. Calling home or even getting a cellular telephone signal was impossible.

By 9:30, the Suffern, New York train (which passes through Allendale, New Jersey) was boarding on track three. The train was delayed so as to accommodate more passengers. Finally, about 9:50, we left the station.

The train was quite crowded and late. People with radios reported that a third plane had slammed into the Pentagon and that there were other commercial jets unaccounted for. Sitting on the train among frightened strangers, thinking of my wife and children, it seemed as if the world was ending. For some of us that day, it did. For the rest of us, the world was irreversibly divided into pre-9/11 and post-9/11. Thoughts drifted to my father, who with a bad heart was seeing this on television and not knowing if one of his sons was okay. I quickly said a prayer to God asking that my father remain healthy through all of this.

At about 10:20, the announcement came: WTC 2 had collapsed. Waves of fear and despair passed quickly from car to car. I offered a nearby commuter a few dollars to use his cellular telephone to call home, which he refused. There were still no signals available to make the call.

Moribund thoughts of my friends and co-workers passed through me. We were testing the computer system at work, and our schedules had been erratic lately. How many of them were at work when tragedy struck?

I thought of the concern my wife, father, brother-in law, and mother-in law would have. I couldn't reach them to tell them I was safe. I considered how the world had changed and the impact on our two young children.

Then my thoughts turned to the relationships I had poorly tended in my life due to family conflicts: my almost nonexistent relationship with my brother and half-brothers. Not once during the September 11 tragedy did they pick up the telephone and ask if I was safe. Later, I would ask my father, regardless of the relationship at the time, would he call if something like this had happened to one of his brothers. Dad said, he would have called his brother. Post September 11th, the relationships with my siblings are on the mend.

On the train, I met a friend, Peter, who I hadn't seen for some time. He, like many of us, wondered what was the point of this act. "I don't get it," he said in shock.

I thought that life was already hard enough and that we didn't need this.

Arriving in Allendale, I called my wife who was in tears and hysterical; I reassured her that I was okay. I also phoned my dad, who at eighty years old has a weak heart. When I called him, he was crying and broken. Before that day, I had never seen or heard my father cry.

I went with my wife to pick up our youngest child at 11:30. Daniel was happy to see me.

A few of the mothers that I knew gave me hugs and expressed concerns about their husbands. Luckily, they were all fine. Although, it was possible to pick up Nicholas as well, we decided not to disrupt his day. We picked him up at 2:30, the usual time.

Many family and friends mistakenly mourned my death that day until they learned of my safety. Watching the replay of the building collapsing on television, I thought of my friends who had perished. I felt guilty being safe and alive. Then about 3 P.M., my manager called and told me that everyone from our area was all right. I was greatly relieved. Although later that night I had a dream about another friend perishing in the attack, she was also fine.

Although many of my friends' 9/11 experiences are private, here are some brief recounts of those who were able to share memories of that painful day.

My friend and co-worker Paula's father was ill and hospitalized with a stroke in New Jersey. As his daughter sat by his side and the towers were burning, he came out of the coma, sat up, stared at the television images and then at Paula, repeated the action, then fell back into the coma. Unfortunately, he never recovered and passed later that week.

A close friend and the father of three young girls who lived out on Long Island, John worked as a data base administrator in the north tower. He was at his desk and largely unaware of what had happened when he saw masses of papers and debris sailing downward past his window. He said it looked like a ticker tape parade. Then he and his friend Paul began to see people jumping from Tower One. While at his desk on the sixty-seventh floor, a huge fireball come streaming down the aisle where he worked. In an instant, he said, he felt every emotion go through him as he dropped his wallet and keys. He eventually made it down the tower to home.

After that day, nothing upsets him.

My good friend and neighbor, Randy, whom I commuted with many days, was on the last Path train from New Jersey into the complex, my normally scheduled train. He passed through the towers on his way to Church Street each morning as so many others did.

Luckily, the train's doors were not opened at the WTC stop. It was 8:50, and two minutes after the first tower was hit. Instead, the train went to the Pavonia Newport stop, where Randy got off, still thinking about getting to his 9:30 meeting.

While at Pavonia Newport, he was directly across from the towers and witnessed the second plane slamming into Tower Two and a ball of flames engulfing it. The afternoon of the tragedy, I stopped by his house. He was drinking rum and told me that he could not shake that picture from his mind. We were all in shock.

Five people on our block, men who went to work or passed through the towers on their way to neighboring streets each day, all survived.

Ferdi (Ferdinand), one of the nicest people that I have ever had the occasion to work for, told of hurling down the stairwells as the building swayed and walls cracked. His wife gave birth to a baby girl later that week. He just kept thinking about his wife and new family and how he needed to survive for them.

Moses, a friend I met on the first day of my new job, worked for the Port Authority. He was on the team of people who built the towers and had a much grimmer story.

His co-workers, high up in Tower One in a conference meeting, were all lost.

The weather was so beautiful on 9/11. The sky was crystal blue, and the air was dry with a temperature of about eighty degrees. The two days that followed were equally as gorgeous. I remember thinking that nature was out of sync with reality. It should be rainy and storming. By Friday, September 14, it finally rained.

I wanted to look for the good in the event, but the initial thought met with much resistance. The little good that I could see was the amount of prayer it generated in this country and the unity locally, nationally, and internationally it inspired. In the following weeks, thoughts about the World Trade Center attack simmered inside of me, and eventually I was able to draw a parallel between our son's birth and the tragedy.

Our first son went through a difficult birthing process, twenty-three hours of labor, being delivered with a suction cup attached to his head, and almost being dropped as he finally made his appearance. The event was painful, stressful, tumultuous, and unpredictable. I realized that the WTC event was a birth of types—a spiritual rebirth on a grand scale. We as a society have grown all too familiar with violent events on television, but it always seemed to be somewhere else. <u>That day the violence came to our door, and we were changed.</u>

While not diminishing the horror, it is good to remember that there were many things that day that could have made it so much worse. It could have occurred at 11 A.M. when the buildings would have been full. There could have been biological weapons onboard the attack planes.

Those first days after the attack, I was like everyone else: mesmerized by the news coverage of this human drama. I watched the network and cable news channels for four or five hours a day and I realized two things: I was becoming addicted and I was being manipulated. Every broadcast on every channel carried a sensational headline: "America Under Attack," "United We Stand," and "America Strikes Back." The language of war was everywhere, and I was helplessly taking it all in. So I began to pull away from the addiction.

I felt the need to pray and decided to go to an ashram in South Fallsburg, New York. I arrived at the grounds after first stopping at my dad's and his wife's place, on Friday. There was a talk in progress by the guru and an evening service scheduled. I prayed, chanted, and meditated. I chanted so much that afternoon my voice grew hoarse and strained.

That evening, just before the service, I wanted to see the sunset in the natural forest setting of Upstate New York. Upon leaving the meditation hall, I walked within a few feet of the guru, Gurumayi Chidvilasananda. While in her energy space, I heard a buzzing sound in my left ear, like that of a radio tuning. I observed the sunset and then returned to my seat. The service continued, and I returned home late that evening. My sleep was deep and restful that night, and in the morning while surfacing from the depths of sleep, I saw the golden white light again. It was September 16th. This time, in a triangle configuration, the golden white orbs were sheathed in a silken clear veil. I was somewhere between deep sleep and consciousness.

I felt that the three shapes in triangle form represented mind, body, and spirit.

The time that immediately followed the attacks was filled with uncertainty. I began commuting to lower Manhattan on September 19th. The voice over the Path system's public address was polite, soothing, and at the same time surreal, as the live person said, "Good morning, today is September 19th. The weather is clear and warm for today, with a chance of showers late in the afternoon." Many people that I used to commute with were no longer on their regularly scheduled trains.

I went into lower Manhattan, via the Path and then to Christopher Street south of Greenwich Village. Using my map from the Internet, I meandered down the streets of New York. About four blocks from my final destination, 80 Varick Street, I decided to cross a particular street that appeared to be closed to local traffic. Entering the barricaded street, two police officers asked for my identification. I felt like a stranger in my own country, that somehow I was in a foreign land, in a police state.

The commute was now one-and-a-half-hours if all went according to schedule. This part of Manhattan was about fourteen city blocks from what was now called Ground Zero, the former site of the World Trade Center.

I believe that the tragedy of September 11, 2001, happened here, in the United States, to make the population at large more aware of the consequences of America's foreign policy. It had become all too easy to flip the channel as various acts of violence were shown to us, somewhere else in the world. As a nation, although mainly good intentioned, we too are tied to the laws of karma like every other individual and nation on the planet.

Post-September 11th, it was difficult to heal. My work area was a makeshift warehouse. I shared a small desk with four people and computers. The closeness to Ground Zero and the background sounds, smells, and dust of the recovery effort were ever present.

The hundreds of families that are forever pained by loss will eventually manifest a greater good, for all, I hope. We don't know exactly how the greater good unfolds, but faith allows us to extend that belief and carry on.

Sadly, in the weeks that followed, services to commemorate the lost were ongoing in all houses of worship in our area. I speculated that within a fifty-mile radius of the attacks there were probably no counties that did not lose residents, and most people in that radius either knew directly or indirectly someone who worked at the WTC complex.

People for a few weeks were noticeably softer in their dealings with each other, even for New Yorkers and New Jerseyians. The fragility of life was at the forefront of thoughts and actions; people were indeed shaken to the core. The notion of "our plan" for life was shattered, for there was clearly a greater plan and force at work.

Even the most tragic events would eventually be shown for the highest good, in time.

As I write this in July 2002, many man-made belief systems are being challenged, forcing individuals affected to grow toward God. Belief in corporate America's integrity has been shaken, and the stock market continues its two-and-a-half-year decline. Corporate greed and economic hardship have us questioning our belief in government at all levels (although I believe we still have the best political system on the planet at this time). The medical industry has been slammed with test results that show hormone therapy could be doing more harm than good in millions of women. Religious scandals are becoming an almost daily event. The holy wars continue in the Middle East as violence escalates, recedes, and then escalates again.

Every man-made system will eventually fail on this planet. Only the eternal, timeless laws and God's will shall prevail.

Six weeks before September 11, 2001, I was sitting at a friend's desk on the fifty-ninth floor of the World Tower Center Tower Two overlooking the Statue of Liberty and the Brooklyn Bridge. Our post-lunch discussion veered into the metaphysical. The gist of the dialogue was: that which you think is permanent isn't; however, that which you think of as temporary isn't.

Translation: Everything we see in the material world, we think of as permanent. But as witnessed by the events of that fateful day, we know firsthand that this is not true.

We, you and I, are eternal—not in this physical form but that of our souls.

What were some of the lasting changes that occurred for me over the tumultuous past two years?

I have a deeper reverence toward life. I am genuinely

softer as a person and see all people as manifestations of God. A feeling of Oneness resounds within me with full awareness that we make each and every experience in our life.

The initial trauma of the 9/11 attacks emphasized for me my path and its importance. I firmly believe that everything is working toward a higher good, even in the face of disaster. I'm a happier, carefree, and more relaxed person.

Relative to the WTC tragedy, I feel as if I've been given a free fifty-year pass for the remainder of my life.

The sacredness of each moment has become more apparent as well as the fragility of mortal existence. I am focused on doing as much good as possible in this incarnation for no other reason than it feels right. Daily I experience new and wonderful mystical experiences.

The golden sunsets and sunrises possess a timelessness and warmth that mirror the golden white light that manifested in front of me. They provide us with a daily reminder of the eternal play in which we all have a part.

∞

PART TWO

PART TWO

Observations

The Miracle of God's Design

There are approximately six billion people on the planet Earth at this time; each is headed in his or her own respective direction in life.

The beauty and precision of the design is that even among the religious, social, cultural, language, and economic diversity, each person is still headed to the same place. That common place is the center of God. This is true, regardless of our individual intentions or lack of belief.

Look back at your own life, its ups and downs, haven't they all played out in a symmetrical flow? We have agreed to or created every experience in our lives for the growth of our immortal soul. The goal of growth is to eventually gain control over every thought, word, and deed, steadily purifying them to get closer and closer to God.

Nothing in this life is a random accident; we are never victims to any experience. We are the architects of all within God's realm. The understanding of karma is an important component to making sense of the sometimes seemingly senseless drama on this physical plane.

If God is omnipresent, then isn't He within us, too?

A Simple and Elegant Design

I have only scratched the surface of the grandeur of the design of the Infinite One. Simplicity and elegance exist at this level; all events bring us closer to the Infinite One. Unpleasant events such as war and crime are even allowed for in the purpose of evolution.

Let's look for a moment at crime and how it can bring someone back toward the One. There are countless cases of hardened criminals "coming to the Lord" as part of their repentance. A criminal act eventually leads to guilt at some level and the need to resolve this guilt. As part of this process, a person opens to other possibilities in life and in turn changes the way he or she thinks of everything, including his or her own existence and the potential of something much larger than oneself.

All things work toward the Infinite One. The beauty of the design is that all things come back to the Infinite One.

Part of the Plan

The Infinite One has arranged our receptor (our brain) in such a way as to have all experiences both positive and negative bring us back to the awareness and harmony of the Infinite One, to lead us back to the center.

Our first priority is to remove the ego and attachment to all things. All of our created difficulties flow from the ego and attachment. Let's take a look at attachment for a moment and its impact on us.

Think about your first new car. Remember the pride of ownership (ego) and how you would protect it, park it in a special place, pay for it. It actually became an extension of you, a part of your ego. You were in effect worshipping it, a car, with the amount of energy you were applying toward it. This type of thinking leads to anxiety, frustration, jealousy (if someone actually had a car nicer than yours), anger (if it was damaged), and many other negative emotions and, ultimately, negative experiences. It is a thing and not an extension of you; it's merely a means of transportation.

An acquaintance once told me he was mortified when his new car, a German import, broke down while on vacation in New England. Apparently, while the German car was being repaired, the family had to make the trip home to New Jersey in a Japanese import. This person told me that they were so embarrassed by being in this type of car and hoped that no one they knew would see them, in such a vehicle, while on the road driving at sixty miles per hour on Interstate 95 South.

The workplace is rife with ego and attachment. Many years ago I worked for an individual who needed to learn to be a nicer person. This person constantly belittled people who worked for him, using his ego to elevate himself and degrade those who reported to him. As he had done unto others, so too was he treated eventually. There were constant ill feelings around him, and no one liked working with him. His shouting, swearing, and fist pounding on the desk tested everyone's patience. This type of abuse is destructive to those around a person, but more poignantly the giver of abuse is frequently punished in a multitude of ways.

What Is Life?

As I mentioned in chapter 1, "The Second Spiritual Awakening," while in a deep meditative state, I asked the question: "What is life?"

From the quiet darkness arose the awareness, "Evolution." Evolution is all we are doing here on Earth, nothing more.

∞

Knowing this, respecting all life on the planet becomes second nature.

There is no end to that evolution; it continually unfolds.

In the Next Steps section in the back of this book, I discuss paths that will continue to assist you in your unfolding spiritual journey. Without my most recent experiences, I would not have been emotionally open enough to help bring this book into reality. I needed to pass large amounts of suppressed pain in order to be able to write from and teach from the heart, a part of my evolution.

In my own evolutionary experience, the intellect first opened to God, then the heart. Once my heart was open to Mother Father God, great freedom and love was attained. My path was clearer than ever.

The answer to "Who am I?" was crystal clear, and the same answer applies to everyone. We are all Mother Father Gods in the making.

We are eternal beings of light and love, evolving endlessly through eons of time.

Make It What You Will
In chapter 3, "The First Spiritual Awakening," I wondered how cause and effect works on this planet. Before I could even properly frame the question, awareness dawned, "Make it what you will."

∞

Through our will, our life unfolds. The more it is in alignment with God's will, the more harmonious and beautiful life will be.

Karma
Karma is often simply defined as cause and effect. Through evolution, we can all witness karma. The rise and fall of civilizations can be considered karma on a large scale. The Western vernacular acknowledges karma—without directly referring to it—with the saying, "What goes around, comes around."

I have been fortunate to recognize karma in many instances in life. It is a real power not only present at the individual level but throughout any structure involving individuals. Organizations, companies, cities, states, nations, geographic regions, and the entire Earth are all subject to the laws of karma.

Here's an example of karma working in the workplace: A coworker decided to slow the progress of a project we were working on. This attitude, in effect, actually slowed the progress of this individual, especially in the company. He was dismissed.

Karma extends beyond the present manifestation and into all lifetimes.

Reincarnation

Without the concept of reincarnation, many occurrences in this world don't make sense. A person hurting another person and appearing to "get away with it" tells us that life isn't fair. The only way of making sense of the superficially random events is to seriously consider reincarnation.

Many of us have had feelings that we had been in a place before or that we experienced a similar situation before. Are these memories of another past?

The Universe Is Object Oriented

You can attain anything that you want in this life through the power of your thoughts. Thoughts are magnetic. Focus on the end result that you want—feel and believe as if it has already occurred. Leave open the possibility that this or something better is now manifesting for you. Meditate on it, and it will be yours.

The mistake that most make of us make in life is that we focus on the negative things in our lives thereby continuing to create and recreate negativity. Have you ever met someone who was either accident-prone or had continual bad luck? Usually within minutes of meeting an individual like this, they will tell you their story, reinforcing their negativity.

The Master said, "Therefore I say unto you, what things so ever ye desire, when ye pray, believe that ye receive them, and ye shall have them" (Mark 11:24).

Thoughts and Feelings Are Things

The energy of thought ripples out through the universe on the invisible pond. The ripples are then returned to the original sender in the form of manifestation. Thoughts have a magnetic quality to them, in that they attract the essence of the thought into our physical reality.

One of the affirmations that I used to bring this book into the light was, "Okay, God, I am willing to let my creative gift explode out into the world." You can make up your own affirmation to help you unleash your potential or free you from your self-made prison.

We live in a house of mirrors. When I was a child, a favorite saying of the time was, "People in glass houses shouldn't throw stones." A more contemporary view of this might be, "We live in a house of mirrors, and all thoughts bounce off the mirror and become part of our reality."

Buddha said, "We are what we think. All that we are arises with our thoughts. With our thoughts, we make the world."

Our thoughts are composed of energy that in turn attracts to us from the ether a like energy resulting in manifestation. So pay attention to what you are thinking.

The Path

The fact that you have read this book this far shows you have the intent to change. Most of the work is getting to this point: the point of intent, having experienced what does not work.

For me, spiritual awakenings or growth occur in a similar way. The pattern goes something like this: I focus on internal body cleansing first by directing myself toward pure foods—fresh vegetables, fruits, and organic products where available as well as plenty of water, juices, and herbal teas. I have removed caffeine, alcohol, and meat consumption from my life. Occasionally, to accelerate the process, I fast for up to three days. You should consult your physician before fasting, and be aware that there are ways to start a fast and to stop a fast that need to be considered. Please consult another source for the mechanics of fasting. The process is marvelously freeing from the regimen of eating, and you have lots of extra time during the day. By purifying the diet, we purify the mind and the emotions making way for other experiences. (Caution: Once again, consult your physician before starting any fast.)

In addition to detoxifying the body, my own path included other elements of cleansing both the body and mind: I removed television and radio from my life. Instead, I read and listened to spiritual discourses and chanting tapes before sleep and in the early morning. The practice of yoga and meditation also were key aspects of my path. Please consult a physician prior to changes in your exercise regimen.

By cleansing the body, we make ourselves ready for spirit.

Naturally, these changes did not occur in one day nor

were they fully implemented on the first attempt. These changes were implemented over several decades with an ebb and flow like that of the tides. However, little by little, the change became the norm and my former way of eating, entertaining, and living became the divergence from the new routine.

The path to unification of body, mind, heart, and soul leads us to the eternal and the understanding that this is a journey and not a destination. We are all evolving to our highest potential as humans. We are all works in progress, masters in the making.

Detoxify the Vessel of the Soul

My view is that we cannot attain a good connection with the Infinite One using a dirty plug. The dirty plug is the body, which needs to be not only clean outside, but also clean inside.

Breathing properly and deeply promotes physical and mental well-being. By oxygenating our bodies, we provide a constant cleansing of all our cells, which is vital to our healthy existence. Most of us are shallow breathers due to years of bad habits. Stresses of today tend to force and cause shallow breathing. Practice consciously breathing deeply using your diaphragm the way it is intended. Inhale deeply and exhale fully. Practice this technique several times a day until it becomes a good habit. When you are not in the moment, you are probably not breathing enough. If you breathe deeply, you will slowly return to living fully in the moment.

Drinking sufficient water is another needed but neglected area of our daily regimen. We need at least eight to ten full glasses of water per day in order to promote health. Be careful of the source of water. Even bottled water may not be as pure as you would like it. Some waters are packaged in glass only, which is preferred so that no plastic leaching occurs.

Drinking alcohol, caffeinated beverages, and gorging on rich foods, excessive meats, and fats can put our body in a state of stress and lack of harmony with what it was designed to consume. We are not truly carnivorous, but herbivores.

If you study the digestive tract of a lion, which is clearly a carnivore, you would observe that the intestinal tract is a fairly straight direct route to elimination, unlike our convoluted human digestive tract. The significance here is that the material in the digestive tract becomes acidic during the process of digestion, which in turn allows for significant bacteria development, thereby promoting much of our present-day digestive problems and diseases. Each year more that sixty-two million Americans are diagnosed with some type of digestive disorder, including cancer.

We need to consider eating healthy foods as much as possible: vegetables, fruits, nuts, and whole grains, preferably certified organic. This healthy diet can include occasional, small portions of chicken, meat, eggs, and fish, again preferably organic. Please be advised to consult your physician prior to changing any diet or exercise regimens to be certain that what you are doing is right for you.

Emphasis needs to be placed on the importance of organic products; they are purer for your body, better for the environment, and taste better. Unfortunately, they will tend to be a little more expensive. Recently, in discussing the topic of organic verses regular pesticide-treated food, I wondered what the implications would be if the local produce aisles in our various markets labeled nonorganic as pesticide-treated foods. I could not imagine that thinking adults would willingly poison themselves and their loved ones.

Our diet is in major conflict with nature's intended nutrients. Due to excess resources, people in the Western world can eat pretty much whatever they want. A number of years ago the effect of diet on health was studied in China. In the agrarian countryside, the dominant diet staple was rice, followed by vegetables and, lastly, meats. When a family of five sat down for the nightly meal, occasionally meat would be served. The portion of meat for all five family members was equal to slightly less than an individual would eat in the West. These Chinese had no diseases typical to Western culture (i.e., heart disease, cancers, obesity, diabetes, or high blood pressure). When these genetically similar people moved to the big city, Beijing, lived a number of years in the city environment, and were exposed to a Western-like diet, they developed diseases comparable to their Western counterparts.

Meditation

The use of meditation, sitting in quietness and listening to the Infinite One, was essential in my journey to spirit. The most effective way that I have found to meditate is to allow twenty to thirty minutes per day for quiet, uninterrupted time. Determine the best meditation time for you: before sleeping or upon awakening. These are optimum times in the day.

Sit in a comfortable position with your back straight (avoid lying down, as you will fall asleep), close your eyes, and breath deeply three times. The three deep breaths are cleansing breaths, cleansing the body of toxins and assisting in the relaxation process. Begin counting backwards, slowly from ten to one, taking a deep breath and telling yourself to relax with each number.

Next, focus your attention on relaxing every body part. Focus on the feet first, then toes, then ankle, moving up the body. Feel each body part relax deeply, and feel the muscles connected to the body part relax and unwind.

Continue moving your attention up your body and tell your legs to relax and feel as if they are relaxed. Next, focus on the pelvic area and relax it. Remember to breathe deeply and continue to count back, slowly. Feel your stomach relax as well as your chest and arms. Now relax your neck, shoulders, and back, breathing deeply and relaxing completely. Finally, feel your face, scalp, and eye areas relax. You should now be completely relaxed.

At this level of awareness, all things are possible; all desires will be fulfilled or lead to something better. Here you will find answers to your questions and healing energy. Any experience is attainable at this level.

In this state sometimes, you will not have awareness of

yourself, but awareness without yourself. The self that your ego thinks of as you will have melted way into the background. You are now connected to the universe, all information and knowledge; all answers to all questions are available to you. This Oneness is always available, but more readily apparent in a meditative state. Practice meditation daily and it will slowly bring about changes in your entire life, from your outlook in life to your diet.

Frequently, when I start my meditation routine, I see concentric circles as my consciousness passes through deeper and deeper levels of awareness. These circles are guides or signposts that we are now engaging our meditative power. Be kind and patient with yourself, and please be aware that individual meditative experiences do vary.

Creative Visualization

Creative visualization is a technique that can be deployed within the process of meditation. Essentially, you paint a picture of that which you desire, and feel as if it has already occurred. You may want to say to yourself: "This or something better will now manifest for me for the highest good of all concerned."

∞

For breaking habits, such as smoking or poor nutritional patterns, focus first on the negative, then cross it out and experience the positive. Use the following creative visualization: The first time, and only the first time, you meditate on that subject, you should see a picture of yourself the way you presently are. Then draw a line through this picture, like the universal symbol for "no." Then smash this image as if it were a mirror.

Awareness is different than linear thought. In the case of linear thought, we are actually walking through the mechanics of thinking, i.e., twelve plus fourteen equals twenty-six. Awareness can be thought of as intuition. Here's another example of awareness: A friend of mine who has trouble remembering details says he tracks down information by asking himself a question and listening for the answer. He often finds himself directed to a book that contains the answer.

My healing experience with my uncle who was deathly ill occurred in a meditative state. I had envisioned two entities surrounded by energy; they resembled cartoon characters who had touched electricity—jagged from the electrical buzz. Next, there was a discharge of my energy to his energy. After this, I fell asleep and awoke peaceful and happy that I had helped in my uncle's healing.

Yoga and Exercise

Exercise is another important area of your life; my personal favorite exercise is hatha yoga. The practice of hatha yoga assists greatly in making the connection between body, mind, heart, and soul.

Yoga is a wonderful outlet for stress and keeps the body limber. An interesting story from yoga class is that of a woman about sixty-five who went to the doctor for her annual checkup. The physical was fine, and the doctor remarked that she was still growing. She had grown a half-inch since the last visit. The following year, the same thing occurred. The practice of yoga, with its emphasis on spinal stretching, caused her to "grow." (Caution: check with your doctor before starting the practice of yoga.)

To read more on this subject, I recommend *Richard Hittleman's Yoga: 28 Day Exercise Plan.* I can assure you that if you follow this course for twenty minutes per day, you will feel completely different, symmetrical, and less stressed. Consult your physician before initiating an exercise program of any kind.

Our modern-day lifestyle takes away from our traditional form of exercise: working in the fields. The great reduction in physical activity contributes to the large amount of disease in our society. Modern medicine is focused on the effect, not the cause of the disease. It is important to physically exert the body a number of times per week, preferable each day, so that the body will cleanse itself of toxins, which are generated as part of the digestive process as well as in our environments. Again, consult a physician to determine what's best for you and your present lifestyle.

Affirmations

Through the use of affirmations, we are able to alter our life experience. Affirmations are especially powerful in creating change and reprogramming our old thoughts and habits, I have frequently used affirmations to facilitate my spiritual growth.

Religion

I have been blessed so much in this incarnation. I had no idea just how much until the awareness dawned that everything is spiritual. There is nothing outside of the spiritual world.

Religion is one of the finest belief systems in the world with so much good flowing from the various sects. In some cases, however, it falls below its best potential. We are all from the same source, the Infinite One. No single religion is superior to any other. It defies all rationality that the Infinite One would have one iota of cynicism as part of Divine makeup.

Imagine on judgment day being told, "Sorry, you were not worshipping the right God!" or "Sorry, you were born into the wrong circumstances" or "Sorry, you worshipped in the wrong place." The idea that the Infinite One has predetermined that certain individuals or energies will never be allowed to attain eternal life is illogical, irrational, and an insult to the Divine.

Unfortunately, human history is filled with holy wars, and many people to this day are killed or sacrifice their life in the name of the God, Allah, or the Infinite One. From a young age, we are told that "their religion" is not the true one or that "their belief system is in error." Many religions perpetuate an us-against-them mentality. After all, in a sense, religions are in competition with one another. Their job is to win you to their side and keep you there.

As a species we need to accept any and all religious belief systems as valid, and not inferior to that of our own. We are all here now, as a part of the plan, and need to recognize this fact. We collectively need to elevate the experience of life on this planet. To add more joy, happiness, and love to the experience on this planet is to have lived.

Faith

Faith in all things is a key to our continued evolution. We need faith and belief when we are meditating. This energy ensures that we will attain the object of our desire or something better for the highest good of all.

We need faith in times of health and in times of sickness.

The Bible notes that "As you have believed, so too is it done unto you," which means you create your own experiences each and every one.

∞

Have faith in the process that all things are working out for the best possible results, in their own time. Many of us cling to the old and refuse to change no matter how miserable a situation might be.

A number of years ago a friend of mine was unhappy with the work environment, which he had been in for more than twelve years. He was being gently pushed from multiple directions at the same time; however, he would not take the cue. The relationship with a new manager was difficult, the relationship with the firm he had worked for and helped build was poor, and even some relationships with coworkers were not as satisfying as they had been. He experienced much pain due to his feelings of being cheated by the firm, which he had helped build. Finally, the end arrived and he left. After leaving, he improved his earnings by 35 percent, reduced his commute time from forty-five minutes to five, got rid of the extremely selfish owner, and improved his work environment by providing more value in a new position.

His entire life became better professionally, personally, financially, and even spiritually, by having a little faith in the unfolding process of life itself.

Goldie

Goldie is a goldfish that lives in a bowl on our countertop in the kitchen. One day Goldie goes out to try to find water. Determined she goes to the bottom of the tank by the gravel, to the top of the tank, and by the plants. Everywhere Goldie looks she can't find water!

Goldie, my dear friend, is you and me before we find God. You see the problem in finding God is that Mother Father God is not in just one place, but everywhere. Like Goldie, we are immersed in God's realm, but we can't "see it."

There are many paradoxes in finding God. Mother Father God is everywhere and at the same time nowhere.

Psychic Power

We all possess some degree of psychic power, and if exercised, it will grow in capability like any other skill or muscle. One of the most beautiful psychic experiences of my life was to view in utero the facial image of our first-born child. His facial profile was and remains a part of me as an adult.

Many other psychic experiences have occurred in my life. In part 1, I discussed "seeing" letters in a closed mailbox and "seeing" the outcome of dice prior to their rolling. I now realize that part of Edgar Cayce's book, *Modern Prophet*, was a psychic connection as well. Now that my emotional side is opened, I also get many psychic feelings or perceptions, in addition to "seeing."

The Sophisticated Modern World

When we consider our modern world and all of its technological accomplishments ranging from the space shuttle, computers, and telescopes to magnetic imaging and genetic engineering, an artificial sense of advancement arises.

Conceptually, consider the lack of degree of understanding of the power of our own thoughts and their interconnectivity. Have you ever bumped into someone you were hoping to avoid? Do you think that it was an accident that you met the very person you wanted not to? The energy of your thoughts and emotions attracted you to this person like a magnet.

The universe, as far as my limited understanding can explain at this time, is like a finely meshed grid of invisible wire. The grid is connected to everything living and nonliving. The wired grid catches our thoughts and feelings and returns the results of our thoughts into our life. Then we say, "I don't know how this happened." Our thoughts made it happen.

Every Experience Is a Lesson

There is an invisible aura around us and with us at all times.

Presently, our ego-driven mind is just about at the end of its capabilities for propelling the human species further, in evolutionary terms.

Our thoughts create our realities. Our consciousness is not simply viewing and experiencing random events that just "pop up." Every experience that occurs in our life is a lesson, which needs to be understood. Until an experience is assimilated and changed into knowledge, it will continue to recur. These experiences require introspection, in order to assess and, if needed, apply corrective action.

On the physical plane, there is a time lag between thought and results or cause and effect. This time lag gives us the illusion of detachment between cause and effect, but remember that cause (thought) creates the results (our experience).

Thoughts always precede our experiences.

Be Here Now, Fully Present

Buddha said, "Do not dwell in the past, do not dream of the future, concentrate the mind on the present moment."

∞

So many of us rush through our days, weeks, and years, and before we know it, life has ended. We can become so focused on the past (what we should have, would have, or could have done), or so focused on the future (what we will do), that we miss the only time we can live—now.

Know that the past is finished, and the future has not yet come. To accomplish anything, we need to exist in the present moment. Our stress level is dramatically reduced when we operate in the here and now. I consider our lack of focus on the present as one of society's greatest mental diseases today.

First, if we are not living in the present, where are we living? Often, we are so focused on the future, we almost completely forget the now. We obsess about the future, how we look, how we are perceived, aging, retiring, etc.

Paradoxically, when the future finally arrives, we begin to obsess in the past wondering, "What was I thinking?" By living out of tense, we are really not living; we are existing in almost a state of suspended animation. We are out of the now and completely out of touch with our body's signals, our true feelings and thoughts.

We are robbing ourselves of the only time we can live—now. In not living in the now, we can make bad choices regarding out diets and habits. We may eat to cover up our true feelings about a subject. We may participate in self-destructive behavioral patterns such as smoking or drinking or worse. Because we are not living in the now, we rationalize that we are more or less not responsible for what happens in the now. We are not in control, we tell ourselves. Avoiding now means I can do whatever I want, because in a way it's not really me engaged in the behavior.

The fact that you're alive now demands that you live in the now completely to be a satisfied human being. The only way you will have peace in your mind, heart, and soul is to live fully now.

Avoiding now is hiding from our self-made difficulties, not addressing the very problems that will allow us to grow. Your problems are your teachers, but if you never attend class, when can you solve your problems? Imagine living an entire life and spending almost no time living it in the present? What a waste of human life.

Your abilities are greatly enhanced by focusing on the present. A good exercise to see where your attention is focused is to "watch" or follow your thoughts during the day. Based upon the daily dialogue that we all have within our own minds, we can monitor and determine where our thoughts (energy) are being directed. Please be aware that it takes a little extra energy during your day to monitor your thoughts. It is possible to be fatigued from the activity of watching one's own thoughts. I recommend doing this exercise for a week to determine where you are living: past, present, or future. After understanding this, you can continue to improve your focus on the present moment.

If you want to observe living in the now, look at nature. Once I watched a blue jay in the process of picking a caterpillar out of a nearby tree. The blue jay dropped the insect, but without missing a beat, it swooped down to the location of the now falling caterpillar. The bird simply plucked the caterpillar right out of the air. The point is that this little creature was so in the moment that it was able to recover from dropping its own meal.

Most of us revel in a refreshing bath. Have you ever wondered why you feel so relaxed and refreshed after taking a soothing soak? Yes, the stresses of the workday are suspended, but more significantly, we are much more focused on the now, the present.

When we are not living out of tense and wasting tons of energy fighting the present, life is pleasant. We can choose to be grounded in the now. Many of us automatically do this during vacations. We enjoy a vacation at the beach and the soothing sounds of the ocean waves churning in and out. Again our senses are not resisting the present; we are pulled deeply into the present moment. Lilias Folan, a wonderful yoga teacher, always said in her program, "Be here now." This is the key to opening a new doorway of experience. We can live in a perpetual state of now, if we choose.

Learn from Nature

Being in nature helps you to find your spiritual path. Nature's beauty and wonder can help bring about new feelings and perceptions.

Nature is perfect in its design and interaction. From the smallest creatures to the largest, there is an interrelationship and interdependency of all life. This could not be an accident, or the product of random evolution. The systems are intertwined and related in a most intricate way.

All life forms are valued within the scope of nature. No life is greater or less than another; they all have worth in and of themselves. Balance, harmony, and interdependency are quite evident.

One beautiful June dew-filled morning I was shooting pictures of roses. During that time, I noticed how the myriad of beautifully colored roses were symmetrically dusted with tiny crystal droplets of water. The precision was stunning, as if an artist had carefully placed each and every dot of water into its proper place. Perfection was apparent in the proportion, spacing, and size of water droplets. The pictures were so good that on another occasion I went to the same place bringing my own mister of water in case I needed to subsidize nature. This particular day was not dew-like, and I used the mist bottle on the roses. Try as I might, however, I could not recreate nature's beauty and symmetry using the mist sprayer.

On an August morning sitting on a rock overlooking a wet grassy area, I noticed a beautiful emerald green spot on the lawn. As I observed the grass with utter fascination, it shimmered in the soft morning light. After staring at it for several minutes, I noticed by slightly shifting my gaze the color would change, tracking the colors of the rainbow from lightest to darkest. I had seen hundreds of dew-soaked mornings, but never observed this phenomenon.

The beauty of a sunset slightly hidden by light cloud cover shows the golden light and streaming grace that is falling on Earth. Nature shouts out the glory and beauty of life every day and everywhere. Take a moment to listen.

∞

From these insights on the design of nature, we can take a lesson about our own dealings with people of all races and creeds. None is greater or less than any other—all are manifestations of the Infinite One. Each person we meet in our life is a reflection of this Infinite Being and should be treated as such.

The workplace should also mirror the harmony of nature and provide for a place for people to interact, cooperate, learn, and grow. Conflicts frequently arise when these rules are violated.

In addition, our dealings with nature should reflect its own proper balance and lack of abuse. The Native American could not understand the concept of selling of land, because it was here before us and would be here long after us. They lived in delicate balance with nature, careful not to destroy the system.

While riding on a train through a largely industrial area with rail lines and warehouses, I saw a series of beautiful pink hibiscus plants growing on each side of a polluted and refuse-strewn stream. The beauty of nature continued to pour through this industrial area, revealing its infusing beauty.

There is no place that you can look and not see God.

Spring

If you have ever truly observed the springtime transition from death to life, you would surely believe that there is a power, which has set all this in motion. I believe spring plays a significant role in the Infinite One's plan, in that from apparent death, life and abundance unfolds.

In the northeastern region of North America, from January through early March, the landscape undergoes a miraculous transformation. The middle of winter is barren, frozen, and colorless, devoid of outside signs of life. Gray skies and stark tree branches abound. As the winter leads into spring, the lifeless outside comes alive. The season starts slowly with small buds on the trees. Next light green growth is evident, followed by explosion after explosion of color and flowers in bloom everywhere unfolding and heralding in the miraculous transformation.

Most of the clues to life are displayed to us in full view; it is only necessary that we quiet our own ego-dominated thoughts, so that we may listen to the awareness surrounding us.

The grand design points to an infinitely wise being. Observe how intelligent plant life is with its leaf, branch, and ultimately plant creation always bending toward the light. This serves as a continual reminder that we too should bend toward the light, with every opportunity in our life.

Look at Your Gifts

Focus your attentions to your daily life in search of your gifts. We all have them. What do you love to do naturally? What do your friends and family members compliment you on or tell you that you're good at doing? These are clues to your special gifts. If you look at your job and focus on the parts that you most enjoy doing, you will find other clues. There are clues all around; just be open to them. Openness is the first step to finding your gift. After that initial step, the next step is revealed, step-by-step. All we need to do is listen to our inner self and follow one step at a time, exercising our faith in the process.

Some of us have a gift of teaching, healing, working with others, helping others find their gifts, a soothing voice, etc. Ask yourself the question, "What are my special gifts?" then listen to your inner voice for the answer. You will receive the answer when it is time. No, we are not speaking about predestination. This is simply a matter of being in touch with your unique skills and being ready for when you should move on to the next step. Imagine a newborn infant trying to run; it is impossible. A child must first learn to move its limbs, then crawl, walk, and finally run. The running part sometimes happens almost as soon as the walking! Still, none of this can be rushed—it happens when it is supposed to happen. So it is with the timing for using your special gifts.

We all need to help as many people in our life as possible, whatever their needs may be. This should be done lovingly and without the thought of reward either apparent or hidden. Make sure your motives are pure and not ego driven, such as a desire to get or maintain control, to brag, or any other negative reasons.

The Infinite One sees through our motivations quite easily, knowing our true heart.

The most rapid evolution of the self is accompanied by tapping into our true gifts or purpose here on Earth. The Infinite One has seen fit that you and I should be here now to evolve within the physical world.

Create a Dream Log

Keep a separate diary next to your bed and begin to log your dreams.

Dreams are teachers. They try to show us where we are stuck in various ways of thinking and acting. Many scientists have awakened to find a problem they have long pondered suddenly solved in their dream state. When we dream, we enter other realms of reality. As you start to accumulate dream information, patterns will emerge and creative solutions to some of your most pressing problems will become apparent. There are several books to aid in the interpretation of dreams. The simple act of logging your dreams will help you remember and learn from them.

You sleep one third of your life, you may as well benefit from the time.

Accept Your Humanness

A number of years ago, I made some errors in business and was initially quite upset at myself. Then in a lucid moment, I received the awareness to "accept your humanness." Naturally, on the physical plane, we are all imperfect, and it is important to understand that errors occur.

I believe that many of us have awareness at some level of our prior perfection and that this is a key reason why we tend to get upset at ourselves when errors occur.

Obstacles Are Teachers

Each obstacle—all pain, all unhappy experiences, all fears, all negativity—is given to us as our teachers. Negative experiences show us face-to-face what does not work. By thinking about the experiences, we can determine the lesson and how to change, so that the experience is more pleasant next time.

"The whole secret of existence is to have no fear," said Buddha. "Never fear what will become of you; depend on no one. Only the moment you reject all help are you freed."

If we look at an athlete training for the high jump, little by little, he progresses to his maximum capability. Each minor failure causes a small change in his technique, attitude, thinking, timing, or execution. Gradually, he achieves the perfection that allows him to jump as high as possible.

In many ways, our life is much like that of the athlete's high jump process, building on our successes and changing to achieve maximum results and eventually perfection.

Make a list of your biggest fears, whether they are related to health, family, environmental issues, financial problems, death, not being accepted by others, whatever you are harboring as your deepest fears.

Look at the list closely, while recognizing that you are eternal, you are love, you are light, and that the Infinite One loves you. With this fully in your consciousness, now how do your fears look? Do your fears now appear trivial, not as relevant as they might have looked a few minutes prior? The fears should now contain less power to hold you.

Creating Your Reality

Whatever you want in this life is available to you, in abundance. In a meditative state, feel as if it has already occurred, see it, and experience it. End your meditation with an affirmation that "this or something better will manifest for me in its own time."

∞

Know that it will occur in its own time. Here's an example of how we make our own reality. In the late 1980s, I had purchased a co-operative apartment in the southern New Jersey area. The unit was nice, large, and carpeted wall-to-wall. Still when it came time to sell the unit, we had difficulty. I visualized myself walking down the driveway on a warm, sunny, spring Saturday, opening up the mailbox, and getting the closing check from our attorney. The reason that I picked Saturday was because that was the only day that I would be home in time to open the mail. Normally, my wife would be home earlier and get the mail for us. Well, after a few meditative sessions focusing on the dilemma of selling the apartment, a series of new ideas came to me. At the time I was riding the train back and forth to work, I picked up the *New York Post* and noticed that the newspaper had a special offer in its classified ads. As long as the seller agreed to reduce the selling price by one percent, every six weeks, the *Post* would continue to run the ad for free. I placed the ad for the apartment, with a slightly higher price, expecting several reductions in the offered price. After about eight weeks, we had several buyers who were interested in the apartment, and one of them eventually bought the unit. Sure enough, one Saturday morning, I walked to our mailbox just as I had done in my meditation, and there was the closing check for the property.

Why Me God?

The Infinite One has put us where we are so that we may learn, experience, and grow. Every adversity and victory is an opportunity to learn and draw closer to the Infinite One.

Gratitude

An emotion that we really need to get in touch with every day is gratitude. We have so much to be thankful for in our lives that we so often forget. Our loved ones, our health, our life on this planet, nature's limitless beauty, the midnight sky, a sunrise or sunset, a breeze on our face, shelter, food, clothing. By connecting to gratitude, we open ourselves to abundance in every aspect of our life simultaneously.

To give thanks to God for everything right and wrong in our life is a step forward. The things that we perceive are "wrong" are just our understanding of how things work. Remember everything is connected to God. Maybe we need to ask, "What am I supposed to learn here?" Take the things that seem to be going wrong as our teachers. This will be difficult to do—unless you are present, now.

Love

The reason for our existence is God's love. Love everything with your whole heart always and you will live in
bliss and joy forever. Acceptance of love is another aspect
of how we open to greater and greater amounts of love in
our life. As the Bible explains in 1 Corinthians 13:13, these
three remain: faith, hope, and love. But the greatest of these
is love.

Be open to all. Love all people, animals, and nature.
Don't leave a single creature or thing out. Make love a
part of your daily routine, as integral as breathing. Greet
everyone with love in your heart, and observe the difference it makes in your life. Witness how it changes
everything and how everyone responds to you
differently. The love of God is omnipresent; there is
no place where it is absent.

What about war? Well, war is God's way of showing
us that we need to be more open to the acceptance of His
love. Looking out on the shimmering light on the ocean,
each little reflective spot is God's love and light beaming
to this little dot in the universe. No, my dear ones, he has
not forsaken us or forgotten us. It is we who have forgotten and forsaken Him with many other gods—named
money, materialism, power, beauty, ego, sex, status. If you
look carefully at a typical day, what do you spend most of
your time thinking about? Take a look and you will be
surprised. There is nothing wrong with any of these things,
in balance, but put God first in all things.

Children

One of my first lucid thoughts is sitting quietly while my first grade class erupted into pandemonium the moment the substitute teacher left the room. I observed the other children throwing objects across the room, running around, shouting, and screaming, and I had a deep awareness of eternity. Everything is for a purpose, I thought.

Anyone who has children can observe the strong influence that media plays on them. Children act out what they see almost on cue. A child sees a violent event, and then proceeds to act it out on his or her siblings or peers. Parents of the child are shocked at the result, respond to the child's actions, and then continue to expose the child to the same negative information.

The time lag for children acting out their thoughts is much shorter than that of adults. Children are more spontaneous and filter much less. This example clearly shows that thoughts are things and that they create action. The child creates his or her reality based upon what he or she observes.

Children are another source for ego, attachments, pain, and suffering. They are their own entities, not a reflection of their parents. You cannot live through your children. I was recently at a boy's baseball league and saw how serious some of the parents were about the event. It was a vivid lesson in how attachment and ego can lead us astray when it comes to our children. We collectively need to let our children be and enjoy their moment, as their childhood cannot be retained.

Children on Loan from the Infinite One

Our children are on loan to us as parents from The Infinite One. It is our job to do all the things that we are duty bound to do, such as feed, clothe, and provide shelter and security. We also have a responsibility to learn every aspect of our children and provide them with the guidance to fully utilize their own gifts. Every person is a unique creature and possesses special talents that need to be utilized for his or her individual good and the highest good of all. As parents entrusted with the Infinite One's crowning creations, we need to really reach down and search for what is good for the child. We must not try to make them clones of ourselves or, worse yet, live through them, encouraging them to do those things that we could not do. We need to also develop a reverence in them and appreciation of life itself and the power, joy, and simultaneous responsibilities that being a human being entails.

Desire, Attainment, and Disillusionment Loop

We spend our lives in what I have come to know as the "desire, attainment, and disillusionment loop." Remember your first car or your first relationship? Your thoughts were consumed by the object or person you wanted. This is the desire stage.

Once we attain the object, it's almost as if the "Is that all there is?" song starts playing in us. The fun was in the goal setting and getting, not in the having stage. Everything we attain is not enough or we want more of it, until one day when we say, enough.

All things in life—whether it is a car, house, relationship, money, or possessions—lose their luster, always. After orchestrating the appearance of hundreds of objects through our will, eventually we realize the futility.

We are attempting to fill an empty space within us with things. Why not attain a goal that will be always new, always filling, always satisfying? That goal is to really know God within us.

Quiet Longing

In the human psyche, there exists a quiet longing, which is innate within all of us. This quiet longing is the longing to return back to the timeless, complete, pure love originating from the Infinite One.

We go about our lives attempting to fill the quiet longing with everything on this physical plane, when it is not possible to fulfill this longing, unless you recognize that the longing is being used to bring us closer to the Infinite One.

Fear

Fear is a powerful energy; it has the ability to manifest that which is most feared by an individual or group.

If you look back over your life, you will find that many times you have brought into your experience a negative event through fearful emotions. You need to guard that which you are fearful of and recognize fear and fearful thoughts before they become so strongly entrenched in your daily thought patterns. A way to reduce fear is to remember to breathe deeply throughout the day. Yes, just simple deep breathing will release stress, and fear is a part of stress.

Every negative emotion is a clue to where we are not properly oriented. Use negative emotions as tuning forks toward God.

Scarcity

There exists a scarcity mentality that pervades the reality of our physical plane.

In the mid-1970s, the entire global economy was shaken by an oil crisis. Projections of $90 per barrel of oil were reported by the oil industry, sometime in the year 2000, if you could buy it at all (part of the projections included running out of oil by the year 2025). The catalyst of the shortage was the Arab oil embargoes of 1973 and 1976.

Naturally, the oil crisis was the fodder of comedians and talk show hosts. Johnny Carson joked in his monologue that he had an inside secret on the next shortage: toilet paper. Sure enough, the message went out to "buy more" toilet paper. Within two weeks, the talk show host recanted the joke, having already actually created the very shortage that he had joked about. This is an example of thought creating reality.

Life is not a zero sum gain, meaning that just because I have something then someone else must have less. The possibility of continual evolution and cooperation is endless, and there never needs to be a loser. There is no shortage or finite amount of enlightenment.

Money

I am sure that many of us know a person (maybe even yourself), who never has enough money. When you speak to these people, they soon tell you of their money troubles. What such people don't realize is that the thought of scarcity creates the reality, which brings about their unhappiness. Life and this Earth are filled with abundance. When a dandelion goes to seed, more than a hundred seeds disburse from a single flower. A single plant creates many flowers. Are you not greater than a dandelion?

An apple tree creates hundreds of apples, and each falls for us to eat. Within each apple are numerous seeds that will grow into a future tree.

The amount of energy from the sun that hits the planet in a single day is enough energy to power the world's present demands for twenty-seven years! We are surrounded by great abundance.

Old mental programming is obliging your image of the world by bringing the picture carried around in your mind into reality. In effect, our mental self is echoing our thoughts outward saying, "Oh, you want a world of scarcity." When we are changing a habit, it takes a greater force to create a new habit. Whenever those old thoughts of scarcity come up, reprogram yourself by saying several times the following: "Great abundance exists throughout God's world." See it in nature; feel it within yourself; believe as if it has already happened.

We need to change our thoughts and words and be thankful for whatever we have (relationships, family, health, youth, experiences, our life, material goods) and whatever our present situation is in life (there are probably individuals who are worse off). *Absolutely True!*

Watch Your Words

Our words are early broadcasts of what will be the future. Our thoughts are followed by words, and words are followed by deed.

Have you ever responded to a friend's invitation with the words "I'll try"? You know that this is essentially an excuse for not doing what we don't want to do anyway. When people tells us "I'll try," they have given themselves the excuse for not achieving what they were telling us they would do.

Relationships

Relationships are key to the development of us all. Several years ago I was working for a difficult Japanese manager whose expectations were quite high. After several near confrontations, I decided to use meditation to help guide and smooth the relationship.

Instead of choosing to micromanage the relationship, I decided to focus on the end result that I wanted. By micromanage, I mean trying to control each and every twist and turn in the relationship. The universe is object oriented, but you must be careful so as to limit your options by choosing to narrow your focal point. In addition, always follow up a meditative thought with these qualifying words: "This or something even better is now manifesting for me." Again, leave your options open for the best possible outcomes.

I realized that the highest compliment that I had ever heard the Japanese manager say was "very wonderful." I went into a meditative state and experienced him telling me that the work that I had done was very wonderful. Many months later he was sitting in his office telling me that I had done a very wonderful job.

Falling in Love
Falling in love with someone new or falling in love again with someone you know can facilitate spiritual awakenings.

This happened to me with my wife-to-be, Jean. It was a warm spring day. I showed up at Jean's apartment with a single rose and off we rode in my new BMW. We spent the afternoon at Aqueduct raceway in Queens, New York. After some of the races, we left and went to the beach. We nuzzled in the duns, drinking champagne from Waterford crystal on a blanket.

Following this first date I needed no others.

Falling in love is a part of the spiritual awakening process because it is the reflection of ourselves that we are actually falling in love with. Usually after a period of days or weeks, a new experience will occur, kind of as a signpost. The signpost is just that, not the Oneness experience but a good start.

As You Think

<u>As you think so is it done unto you</u>. Our expectations create the reality; <u>we are the engineers of our life experiences</u>. One company came up with the idea that it would offer compensatory time off to consultants who worked extra time, instead of paying overtime. A few contractors were not happy with the arrangement and mistrusted the company. They acted as if they were going to get terminated at the end of the project and used up all the time whenever they could. Sure enough, when it came time to reassign the consultants, those who thought they were going to get terminated at the end of the project were right. They acted out the worst-case scenario, which they thought would occur.

<u>The lesson here is to focus on what you want</u>.

Throughout my work life, I have had the opportunity to work with some difficult managers, and these experiences have taught me quite a bit. Although I did not care for them as people, I still served them as best as I could, knowing that <u>we really only have one Master</u>.

One such manager, whom we will call Jim, was a middle manager in charge of a number of computer projects. Jim was extremely arrogant, nasty, and belligerent. He treated others as if they were ignorant and he was brilliant. Since I had previously worked for a competitor, he saw me as both an enemy and a threat.

Throughout the project, he had lobbied to have me fired. Each time he would push my direct manager to have me fired, my manager would say fine, "but who is going to finish the project?" And each time, Jim would back down from his request. Finally, the project was successfully completed, and months later Jim was scheduled to be moved to another area. Most of us were happy to see him go.

However, his fate had taken an unusual turn in two regards: first, his son-in-law had been hurt in a work accident and Jim was nobly paying the family's expenses. Secondly, instead of being transferred as he had been told, Jim was fired. He'd been caught cheating on his expense report for a dinner involving his area vice president. His son-in-law's injuries from falling off a roof were so severe that they quickly depleted the family resources. Jim had turned to desperate measures to solve his financial problems. Many years later I learned that Jim was selling products and no longer was the boss over anyone. I believe that he needed to learn to treat people nicer and was forced into a role in life that would allow this to occur.

Viewing the Higher Self

In a meditative state, I was privileged to view my higher self. I was not attempting to attract any particular energy or response or focus on any topic. I was simply experiencing a wonderful yoga session when I was allowed to view my higher self. What I saw was a beautifully pure color purple, the most brilliant purple I have ever seen. The scene was depicted in a horizon-like setting, a foreground of black semicircle and a background of a purple horizon filling the remainder of the horizon. Remember that when you meditate, some of your most satisfying spiritual experiences will happen when you least expect them. The point is to show up at meditation with an open and loving heart. Let the rest happen. You may have to meditate for sometime before something "happens," some connection is made. Be patient.

Time

Time is an illusion created for our understanding of the birth to death experience. Eternity has no similar concept of time; there is no beginning and no ending.

Listen to the Quiet Voice

It has been my experience that all of us from time to time experience the quiet voice within ourselves. Some people call this voice intuition. It is a subtle feeling, perception, or awareness.

If we choose to listen to the quiet voice within each of us, we will observe that with each experience we are being subtly guided. By quieting the ego's constant chatter and "I told you so's" in meditation, we can clear our conscious mind and be receptive to awareness. If you ask a question of yourself while in this state, you are likely to receive an answer via awareness, a perfect response to your question or specific issue.

At various times in my work, I have been presented with a challenging problem and found the answer with the help of my quiet voice. After systematically reviewing each aspect of the problem and failing to uncover the root of the issue, I would ask, "What could be causing this?" Frequently, I would receive a "look here" message in the form of an awareness, which would lead me to a solution. If I avoided, dismissed, or ignored the quiet voice, eventually after much effort and frustration, I would be back to exactly where I was prompted to look in the first place.

Unfinished Business

A few years ago a friend and manager had an uncle who had advanced Alzheimer's disease, which left the uncle almost nonfunctional. He had spent the later years of his life with his wife, who also had suffered from the same disease. She had died several years earlier of advanced Alzheimer's, a fact that her spouse was unaware of due to his own condition. He had an atrophied brain, was eating with the assistance of tubes, and had a bad habit of hopping up and down repeatedly, in place. His Alzheimer's condition was slowly deteriorating, as was his quality of life. The physicians who were caring for him were quite amazed that he was still surviving, although not particularly well.

My friend met with the medical staff to discuss his uncle's situation, and the question was raised: Did his uncle have any unfinished business? As my friend began to think about it, it occurred to him that his sick uncle didn't really know that his wife had passed on. In discussing it, one physician recommended that a priest and nun visit the patient and tell him of his loss. Initially, the uncle was startled by the sight of the clergy, but did recognize their garments. They proceeded to explain to him that his wife was dead and was "waiting for him on the other side."

That evening, in his sleep, my friend's uncle died. He apparently was holding on for his wife. Having no other earthly business, he passed on.

Birth and Death: East vs. West Significance

Birth and death, those significant events in life, are handled quite differently in the East and the West. In fact, they are handled exactly opposite by a number of civilizations. As is known in the Western world, we celebrate the birth of a new person and mourn their perceived loss. I say perceived loss because this world is the illusion; the remainder of the universe is reality. The strong attachment to corporeal life is normal, as this is many people's view of "all there is."

Eastern cultures—the Indians, Chinese, and a number of other civilizations—celebrate the death of a person because their view is that this world is full of pain and suffering—in effect, hell. They celebrate the release of your soul from its earthly boundaries and its return back to the Infinite One.

Which view is correct, the Eastern or Western beliefs? Part of me says that the age of Eastern civilizations has something to do with their beliefs. Also, the Western world has always had a more immediate worldly view. Today's life in the material world emphasizes now, hedonistic pleasures, success, money, entertainment, convenience, get all you can as quickly as you can, narcissism, conspicuous consumption, and implicit damnation if you are not materially wealthy. A large part of these beliefs are propagated from Madison Avenue advertisements. An individual's position in life has no bearing upon the value of his or her infinite soul. We are all equals as witnessed by being on this physical plane together.

Meeting My Angels

In March 2000, after imbibing a book by Belinda J. Womack titled, *Angels Guide: A Spiritual Toolbox for Using Angelic Guidance in Everyday Life,* I found myself seated in Belinda's living room, attending a two-day seminar, in Warwick, New York.

I had read most of the book and listened to the compact disc for several months, while at work on the computer.

During the seminar, we explored many aspects of spirituality. One of the exercises was to find out our angels' names. We went into a meditative state, during which time I asked my angels the question, what are your names? An answer in the form of a whisper returned, that was so subtle and quiet that my conscious mind barely registered it. After the meditation, Belinda asked me what were my angels' names. I said, "I don't know." She told me that she thought that I knew, then she mentioned the names Martha and Jake. I recalled hearing their names during the quiet time.

Belinda told me that my last incarnation was in Atlantis. She also mentioned that the left half (emotional side) of me was still very much grounded there. Like many people, I have always had a quiet fascination with the subject of Atlantis. In fact, in one of Edgar Cayce's books, he recounts the destruction of the first Atlantis. Many ideas of freedom are ideas that were based in ancient Atlantis.

I noticed that I felt different a few days before and after the course, as if I was getting a psychic adjustment. Belinda explained later in a private conversation that I was highly psychic and that the pain that we experience is a blessing in disguise. I've noticed that, in my life, pain instinctively has brought me closer to God, as I was unwilling to believe that that's all life had to offer.

Many months later, while commuting on the train coming home in June 2001, I had a vision of a beautiful angel. The angel was female. As I came up from a meditative state, she smiled at me broadly. She was dressed in finely tailored golden clothing; her skin, face, and hands were also golden. The hue was a deep golden color the same as the gold white light that I had seen on my desk earlier that year in April 2001, the same color given off by the early morning and late daylight sun, when the shadows are quite long. I later learned that this angel was the female version of the Archangel Gabriel, or Gabriella. There was a beautiful golden circle, intricate in design and detail behind her head. At first, I thought that this might have been my mother, but later found out who it actually was.

The message that Angel Gabriella had was that she wanted me to help people in their careers.

I now had a visit from an angel, one of God's own messengers, requesting me to help on the earthly plane. The time span between the birth of our children and the writing this book has been punctuated with huge spiritual experiences—direct connections to the Divine and not just speculation, but absolute proof of something much deeper and more profound than most dare to dream. Those experiences continue to unfold and shape my life daily. The longest continuous block of time immersed in a Oneness experience was now two weeks; the connections were growing stronger. More significantly, I could tell that all of the various experiences that I was having had a deeply rooted spiritual connection. There is a realm beyond the physical, and I could connect to it through meditation, thoughts, and feelings on a regular basis. This realization

121

strengthened the experiences and deepened my commitment to spiritual practices.

So now I knew of angels, their existence, and their message and that they too are real and part of God's own energy to assist us on the trip back to God. The trip back is something that we are all attempting to understand and continue. Our life is as brief as a flower in nature, when comparing this time to eternity.

Once I had learned their names, I occasionally asked my angels for their help. I asked for assistance from my angels, prior to sleeping, to meet a challenge I was having at work. My angels answered my request. During the evening and upon awakening, I became fully aware of what I needed to do to solve the problem. Later that single act would clear the way for all other solutions that followed. Upon arriving at the office and considering the suggestion, I could see the simple genius of the solution. The solution to the problem was clear, and the remainder of the work flowed with simplicity.

So angels are available to us and will help us in virtually every aspect of our life. *absolutely!*

The ancient promise, "Ask and you shall receive," was again fulfilled. It required faith and belief to activate the great unseen energy.

When activating your own faith and belief to help solve present problems, rely upon your own angels. Even if you don't learn of their names, trust and believe. The solutions are quite elegant and do not move through the normal linear process, but seem to jump to the essence of the matter. Often more than a single problem is resolved in the process.

Every aspect of your life can be and will be improved.

A Walk in New York City

In a brief fifteen-minute walk on the streets of New York City, I discovered a multitude of ways to make a difference in the lives of others. The first person I met was a young man asking for directions. I gave him directions to Broadway and promptly wished him good luck on his interview. He turned to me in some surprise, because he hadn't mentioned anything about an interview. Somehow, I just knew that was his purpose.

As he walked away, I noticed that his head was down. I caught up with him and walked with him a bit, relaying a little story on positive thought. I told him about going to the carnival with my family. My youngest son asked me to win him a basketball. I started to tell him that, "Oh, Daniel, Dad is really not . . ." but I caught my words in mid-air. Instead, I said, "Daniel, I'm the best basketball player in the world." And that day it proved true. By the time I arrived at the booth, I was pumped and promptly put two swish shoots in, back to back.

I told the man that with each step of his trip he needed to think that he is the best at whatever he was applying for. Our lives had intersected for a purpose beyond mere directions; I felt I was meant to aid him on his own path. At the same time, it taught me the power of our thoughts.

On that same afternoon, I provided directions again. This time to a gentleman guiding a tour of junior high students through the World Trade Center and needing directions to the A train. I helped a young mother maneuver herself and a stroller through an electric doorway. And I assisted another woman when she dropped her magazine.

The point is that there is always a way to serve other people, with kindness and grace.

Affirmations

THESE AFFIRMATIONS ARE DESIGNED FOR YOUR REFLECTION ON A DAILY BASIS. Select one from the list below (or make your own) and work with it until you feel it's time to move on to the next one.

These are repeated as a prayer—see, feel, and believe it as if it has already occurred. Notice the absence of negative words in the following affirmations. Affirmations should be expressed in a positive manner.

God is opening my heart to divine love so that I may reflect that love to many, many people.

Thank you, God, for this day. Help me glorify Thee in each and every way.

Abundance in all things is reflected in God's world, of which I am a part.

Every day in all ways every cell, tissue, organ, and system is getting better.

My life is filled with joy, freedom, abundance, generosity, and compassion.

God, please bring me to Thy will.

I am releasing control of my life to God's divine love and will.

Through God, I create every thought, feeling, and experience of my life.

Every event in my life is to teach me something for my own evolution.

God's generosity is unending and everpresent.

My world is filled with ethics.

I have eliminated anger from my personality.

I take joy in constructive and helpful actions.

God's compassion is boundless.

I now have everything that I need in great abundance.

Glossary of Terms

Affirmations — Positive thoughts and feelings used to dispel the negative tendencies of humanity. Continued use of affirmations will manifest the reality desired or something better. Affirmations are a form of a prayer.

Buddha — The spiritual leader who founded Buddhism in approximately 500 B.C.

Chakra — An energy center in the body. There are seven chakras.

Crown chakra — The highest energy center in the body and associated with purple light.

Edgar Cayce — The Irish psychic known as "The Sleeping Prophet" was born in 1877. He founded the Association for Research and Enlightenment, Inc. (A.R.E.) in Virginia Beach, Virginia, in 1931.

Guru — The spiritual head of a group of followers. Presently, Gurumayi Chidvilasananda is the head of the Siddha lineage.

Karma — The result of each thought, word, and deed.

Kundalini energy — The energy that travels up and down the spine.

Mother Father God — God, both the divine female and divine male energy. Also, the Infinite One.

Oneness — The deep feeling, awareness, and belief that everything is interconnected.

Spiritual awakening — A profound spiritual experience that results in a life change, mystical in nature.

Yoga — An ancient form of exercise to provide symmetry of the body. This exercise fuses the mind, body, and spirit connection.

Next Steps

PLEASE REREAD THIS BOOK ONE MORE TIME to gain the maximum benefit then consider making use of the following resources for furthering your development.

If rereading doesn't appeal to you, review the infinity notation references in the book as often as you like (see index). You could use it as a daily reference.

Consider the following books and courses:

Angels Guide: The Spiritual Toolbox for Using Angelic Guidance in Everyday Life by Belinda J. Womack

The Diamond Cutter: The Buddha on Strategies for Managing Your Business and Your Life by Gesha Michael Roach

"In Search of the Self," a Siddha yoga course available through 845-434-2000 extension 1900.

Richard Hittleman's Yoga: 28 Day Exercise Plan by Richard Hittleman

Please consult a physician prior to any change in exercise or diet programs.

Conversations with a Friend

A DEAR FRIEND AND NEIGHBOR OF MINE, RANDY, AND I HAVE BEEN DISCUSSING SPIRITUALITY at various times such as on the morning commute. Our discussions often focus on the difference between the material and spiritual world and how confusing it is to balance our lives between these worlds. Here are a few excerpts of those conversations:

On the Need to Feel in Control

Randy: I have a problem with spiritualism vs. materialism, the need for German cars, and the need to live in such and such a town.

John: I drive a German car because I believe it is the safest on the road, and I live where I live because we've lived there for more than fifteen years and it has a great school system. My instinct tells me that God doesn't need us to be miserable living on this earth in order to be more spiritual. We need to humble ourselves to Mother Father God's divine will.

Randy: I feel as if I need to control the timing of transitioning to a more spiritual life. I am really not ready to change a lot of things. I have a multiyear plan.

John: Have you ever driven to the airport for a flight yourself?

Randy: Yes.

John: Have you ever taken a limousine to the airport for a flight?

Randy: Yes.

John: Which do you prefer?

Randy: The limousine.

John: By putting God first in your life, you are taking the limousine to the airport with God as the driver. It's a lot better than running around and trying to drive yourself. Life is so much simpler.

Randy: But I still feel the need to control and manage my life.

John: We in the Western world have the use of the mind backwards. We think that we are supposed to figure out and control everything in our life. The mind should be quieted by meditation and other techniques, so that it is open to receiving God's messages and impressions. We don't have to micromanage our life. God will handle the details and, in doing so, reveal how we fit into Mother Father God's plan. By removing the conscious mind (the barking dog), we can start to listen to God.

Randy: When I was younger, I kind of felt on my path. I read books about philosophy. But, now after all these years, I am so far away from my own path.

John: A lot has happened within the last forty plus years: college, jobs, family, children, houses. You can get back to your path starting today.

Randy: But I feel as if I have missed my purpose in life.

John: No, you can still fulfill your highest purpose. Maybe a big part of your purpose was to have children and grandchildren. You are the central figure in the family now and that's important. Part of fulfilling your purpose is to let go of your control. Yes, at first it's a little like driving without your hands on the steering wheel.

Randy: I've been a little depressed lately. Things are not going that well at work.

John: That's a good thing! You are in for some growth-oriented changes. I think that you are concerned about your three-year plan regarding retirement.

Randy: You know, your right.

John: You are unwilling to let go of the control of your plan for retirement. You will always have food and a roof over your head. So what's the problem?

Randy: I guess I just don't want to change my plans.

John: Well, maybe you will get something even better, if you let change in.

Randy: I'm still having problems sleeping straight through the evening. I wake up and watch television, then go back to sleep.

John: The first night I read the "In Search of the Self" course, lesson one, before sleeping, I had the best night's sleep in many months, even years. I knew that many of my suspicions about life were true. (See Next Steps for additional information.)

Randy: Little by little, I'm feeling more comfortable about my three-year plan not working out as I planned. I have been suppressing the uncomfortable feeling about it.

John: That's good, the letting go.

Randy: Yes, I can tell that by the feeling that it's liberating to let go of some of the control. By speaking with you, I notice that I am changing. Gradually, the puzzle is starting to make more sense.

John: It's the energy vibrations that are helping to bring you into alignment. In addition, things that you have been feeling and thinking for a long time are starting to make sense.

Randy: I still have trouble with the materialism vs. spiritualism thing. Although, I do notice that nothing material satisfies that pain we were talking about in my gut. Something may cover the pain for a little while but then it comes back.

John: Well, Jesus said, "Look at the birds, does my Father not provide for them? Are you not greater than they? He knows what you need before you do." I think the point here is God knows you need a roof over your head, meals to eat, clothes, etc. However, you are not supposed to worship, idolize, or put first anything other than God. Eventually, God's will will be done as in the "Our Father" prayer.

Jesus also said, "With all thy getting, get understanding." If I may interpret, He knew that we needed to get things in our life, to survive. But, His emphasis is on our understanding. I believe Jesus meant don't let the getting (of things) cause you to miss the whole point of this life.

Nature shows us that God's world is filled with abundance and so are we. Abundance is not something that conflicts with spiritualism; it's an integral part of it. I don't view them as exclusive. The idea of if I have material goods, then I must not be spiritual doesn't make sense. Regarding heaven, Jesus said, "It is easier for a camel to pass through the eye of a needle than for a rich man to enter the gates heaven." I believe that we need to avoid worshipping money and materialism.

Randy: Yes, but what about free will?

John: We all have free will. We are free to try life our way—the way of pain, suffering, and fear—or we can try it God's way with joy, freedom, and happiness. We all have free will to do as we choose every moment. God's will will be done. It's not a question of if, but a question of when. Mother Father God's will is supreme, but we always have a choice. Randy, I am really happy the way things worked out for my plans in the stock market (a significant monetary loss). I realized that all I was really looking for in my own limited view was a slightly "nicer jail." Maybe a little bit bigger than my present one with a little better food. But instead, through Mother Father God's divine providence, I was truly able to change everything. Everything changed for the better and in ways that I didn't realize I even needed.

On Acknowledging and Listening to Your Quiet Voice

Randy: I noticed that I'm not happy lately with my words. I say things, and they make no sense to me. I want to control my words more. Not what we are presently talking about, but other things in general. My family talks and talks and talks, and I love to listen to them.

John: Yes, but what they are talking about is really just the movie of life, the drama. They say nothing of any lasting significance. Eventually, you will get tired of listening and move to a quieter place in the house. I find myself no longer at all interested in those conversations or television. In fact, if the television's on, I leave the room.

Randy: I have this inner feeling that yoga or tai chi is good for me and would help me in my development. Periodically, it comes up and I keep putting it off because I don't have enough time. I suppress it.

John: How long have you had that feeling?

Randy: About three years.

John: That's the quiet voice or God's will trying to guide you to something that would help put you on your path. That's great! I would recommend Richard Hittleman's twenty-eight-day yoga book. By committing just twenty minutes per day, after twenty-eight days you will feel symmetrical and fluid. That free feeling will help you to be more in touch with your own inner feelings. After doing the twenty-eight-day course, your body will demand yoga periodically to reduce tension and improve flexibility. (See Next Steps for additional information.)

On When to Start the Spiritual Path

Randy: I'm at a good time in my life to start the spiritual path. The children are grown up, college is paid for, etc.

John: Now is always a good time to start. Spiritualism makes all of life easier, not harder. Spiritualism lightens our load. If everywhere you look is a manifestation of God, then there is nothing separate from Mother Father God. There really is no such thing as materialism. We have been inculcated in a wrong way to think that there is something separate from God. There is not a single place where you can look where God does not exist. Everything "material" is part of the kingdom everywhere you look. We in the United

States are much more spiritual than we presently realize; every manifestation here is through the use of our will. We have manifested so much on this plane. We in this country are spiritual, due to the abundance that we have manifested in our lives. This is not to say that the lack of abundance is nonspiritual either.

Randy: I can't believe how much you have recovered in the last month. You really looked bad, and I was worried about your health.

John: Yes, you're right it has been a miraculous transition. What you witnessed was the death of the old John. The old path for me has been transformed into a new path, one filled with joy and freedom.

On Fear

Randy: I have such fear over my three-year plan not being completed. I am also concerned about my wife and children as a result of not finishing the plan.

John: You don't think that if you lose your job, you'll lose your wife and children, do you?

Randy: Well, yes, you know I sat down and laid out the plan where we would not need to count our pennies during retirement. Now, to go back and say that it would not work out that way could create some serious problems. I was listening to a Bob Dylan song and he said something really frightening in the song, "Just when you think you've lost it all, you find out you have more to lose."

John: You need to let go of those fearful thoughts. What about meditating on the problem people and focus on receiving their highest accolade? Like I did, when I first undertook a large project a few years ago for a Japanese company. I studied my Japanese manager, found out what his highest compliment was (which was "very wonderful"), and then in a meditative state visualized him telling me that the computer system that I did was very wonderful. I did this meditation for a couple of months, until I felt that I had done enough. About one-and-a-half years later, he announced that the system that I did was "very wonderful." Randy, you can do this, if you believe you can.

Randy: Well, I'm not sure that I can believe I can do it.

John: My wife mentioned to me last night that I had changed since we were married. So, I asked her, can't people change? She said, "Yes, but you've changed a lot." And I asked her: "Haven't you changed?" She said she hadn't. When we were first married, I was this guy who was going to make a lot of money. I created a situation in which I lost a lot of money in the stock market; I realize that I had to go through that to evolve and feel the losses that I never acknowledged in my life. Since then, money has lost much of its significance for me.

Randy: Well, you never really had this money. It was just a number on a statement.

John: Well, to my wife, broker, and me it was real.

139

On the Connection to Oneness

Randy: You look kind of beat lately, down from where you were a few weeks ago.

John: Yes, I am feeling the loss of the connection to Oneness. Just last night while going to my older son's baseball game, while walking on the field, I had the beautiful sense of Oneness. The beautiful green carpet spread out before me along with the white clover flowers. All at once, there was no me, just the beauty of the white clover everywhere. I thought, how generous God is to have populated this field with so many flowers. It was a real tangible blessing.

Randy: Oh, you mean you lost that connection that you were feeling recently?

John: Yes, I am still in the process of emotionally opening up to the connection and how it comes and goes. Just last night, I had meditated on the experience of Oneness. I think that the meditation was answered by the experience of walking in the field. Dreams, reality, and mediation are starting to converge.

Randy: I think that it's good to let your readers know that the feeling will come and go.

John: Yes, I agree.

Randy: I think that for you and I, it's possible to be on this path having materially attained most of what we wanted.

John: I am not sure if it is necessary. But, my feeling is that in the last ten years of my life, I will have nothing material. This is to allow me to focus on the spiritual side exclusively.

Several months after our first talks...

Randy: Wow! I feel a lot better about work and my three-year plan. I am no longer so concerned about losing my job.

John: You look a lot better, and you seem lighter.

Randy: I had a dream the other day about work. I made a mistake, and they fired me because of it. Then, the very next day that dream came true in that I screwed up. I made a small mistake that was blown up into a medium-sized mistake by my political adversaries.

John: Your dream was a premonition of reality. Remember we had talked about my precognitive dreams and foretelling the future.

Randy: Yes! That's kind of scary. I mean that I could have a dream and that it is tapping into something more than is apparently there.

John: You created the dream, the small error, and even your political enemies. There is a lot more going on here than most people would believe. The mind can't really conceive of the ultimate truth and, therefore, will not relinquish the illusion of its control. The mind and ego create problems or dramas to justify the ego's existence. It shows an individual: "See, you need me."

Randy: You mean I did all that?

John: Yes, at a subconscious level and beyond, you engineered the entire thing as a lesson, to show you that your worst fear is not that bad. Also, the fear is attracting energy to you, creating your reality just like a magnet drawn to you through your thoughts,

Randy: Well, I am also getting a lot of support from my children and wife. Also, if they fire me, then they have to pay me some kind of severance package, maybe two years salary. But, knowing me I would still be upset about the eight or nine months that I missed.

John: Randy, if you can collect two years' salary for not even showing up, I think you will be happy probably the next day, once you get through the shock.

Randy: I noticed my behavior had recently changed at a few parties. I felt like the "master of my game." I got a little cocky and also was into judging people. Then smack, I got hit with this issue at work.

John: The ego and mind got out of control, so you created something to make them step back in line.

Randy: Although I feel better about the fear, it's not completely gone.

John: That's normal; its unwinding. The feeling doesn't just disappear, but slowly dissipates unless we give it more energy with thought and feelings.

Eventually this mind- and ego-based reality will ⟵
collapse on a large scale. The consumer-driven society will end, and the concept of gaining something from an external thing will be as foreign as
the horse and buggy. The search to satisfy something "inner with something outer" will end.

Randy: That's a profound concept: the inner will no
longer be satisfied by something outer.

Addendum

Counseling Services

THROUGH THE YEARS, I HAVE HELPED MANY PEOPLE in their chosen profession or in seeking a new profession, with soulful career counseling. There is probably nothing more draining or frustrating than to be in a position that doesn't fit who we are.

I have also aided many people through difficult times in life.

I have helped in the interview process providing coaching as well as offering advice on various techniques, while job searching. The results have been favorable and often provide a better position than the original sought after.

Here's what a few clients have said.

An actual e-mail from a client, in response to the question how is the new job:

A dream, people are incredibly nice and I'm reporting to the director. No stress, John; these people are crazy. In these days no after 5 P.M. or nothing like that. I love it! I thank God for his blessings; I did say the prayer you gave me every day and still do now. Thanks for being there for me when I was down and broken.

Thanks again, VB

Some comments from someone who secured a position after following some of my advice:

John definitely helped both with confidence and through the interview process. I finally secured a position after following some of his advice.

Another satisfied client:

I would not have got the job without your help!

The rates are reasonable and come with a satisfaction guarantee.

Index

Affirmations 77, 87, 103, 111, 125–26, 127
Angels 120–22
    Archangel Gabriel 121
    Gabriella 121
Association for Research and Enlightenment, Inc. 127
Atlantis 120
Attachment 71–72, 106, 119
Awakenings 14–15, 33, 42, 113, 128
    encouraging 78–79
Awareness 98, 117
    vs. linear thought 85

Baba, Sathya Sai 30
Being in the present 93–95, 104
Biblical references
    1 Corinthians 13:13 105
    John 14: 27 14
    Luke 11: 9–10 16
    Mark 11:24 76, 89
    Prov. 4: 7 16
Birth and death
    how they are handled in the East and West 119
Body cleansing 78
Breathing 80
Buddha 77, 93, 102, 127

Carson, Johnny 110
Cause and effect 92
Cayce, Edgar 13, 90, 120, 127, 128
Chakra 23, 41, 127
Change
    encouraging 78–79
    fear of 18–20
Chidvilasananda, Gurumayi 42, 61, 127
Children
    and ego and attachment 106
    and negative thought 106
Christ-Buddha energy 49, 62
Control
    letting go of 131–36
Counseling services 145
Creative visualization 85
Crime 70

Darshan 42
Desire, attainment, and disillusionment loop 108
Diet
    and cleansing the body 78, 80–82
    vegetarian 41
Dream log 101
Dylan, Bob 138

Ego 17, 18, 19, 38, 48,
    71–72, 106, 116, 141
Emotion
    negative 109
Evolution 35, 70, 73, 89,
    100, 110
Exercise 86

Faith 89
Fasting 78
Fears 19, 102, 109, 138–39
Folan, Lilias 95
Free will 135

Gifts 99–100
    helping children find their
    107
God's design 69–70
Gratitude 104
Growth
    goal of 69
Guru 42, 127

Habits
    breaking with creative
        visualization 85
    reprogramming 87
Higher self
    viewing 116
Humanness
    accepting our 101

Infinity notation 19, 35, 37,
    49, 65, 70, 73, 74, 76, 77,
    85, 89, 93, 97, 103
Intuition 85

Karma 37, 46, 69, 74, 127
Kundalini energy 127

Love 105

Meditation 33, 34, 39, 41,
    48, 61, 76, 78, 83–84,
    103, 112, 116, 132, 139, 140
Money 135
    and the thought of scarcity
    111

Nature
    learning from 94, 96–97
Negativity
    creating 76

Obstacles
    as teachers 102
Oneness 15, 18–19, 65, 84,
    113, 128
    losing the connection to 140
    obstacles to 17

Prayer 61, 125, 127
Psychic experiences 34, 90
Purpose 133

Quiet longing 108
Quiet voice
    listening to 116–17, 136–37

Randomness 18, 69, 75
Reality
    creating 103–4
Reincarnation 75
Relationships 112–13
Religion 87–88

Scarcity 110–11
Siddha Yoga 42, 127
Spiritual guides 17
Spiritual path
  starting 137–38
Spiritualism
  vs. materialism 131–36, 137
Spirituality 17
Stearn, Jess 13
Stock market
  as spiritual teacher 43–49

Thoughts
  creating 29
  creating reality 92, 110,
    112, 114–15
  energy of 77
  linear 85
  monitoring 94
  negative 38, 46, 76, 106
  positive 123
  power of 36–37, 76, 91

Unfinished business 118

Visions
  golden orb 49, 62

War 70, 105
Womack, Belinda J. 120–21
Workplace
  ego and attachment in 71
  karma in 74
World Trade Center
  as spiritual rebirth 60
  attack on 51–65

Yoga 35, 39, 41, 78, 86, 128,
  136

"Angel Guide : A Spiritual toolbox for using Angelic Guidance in Everyday Life." Brenda J. Womack